COGNITIVE BEHAVIORAL THERAPY

HOW TO CHANGE

NEGATIVE THOUGHT PATTERNS

DAVID SANDUA

Cognitive behavioral therapy: How to change negative thought patterns.

eBook & Paperback Edition.

"You can't stop the waves, but you can learn to surf."

Jon Kabat-Zinn, scientist and writer

INDEX

I. INTRODUCTION

Cognitive Behavioral Therapy (CBT), stands at the forefront of clinical psychology as a evidenced-based therapeutic approach that targets negative thought patterns. By systematically addressing distorted cognitions and maladaptive behaviors, CBT aims to restructure cognitive processes to foster lasting changes in emotional responses and overall well-being. This essay delves into the core principles, methods, and empirical evidence supporting the efficacy of CBT in modifying negative thought patterns. Through a critical analysis of key figures like Aaron Beck and Albert Ellis, the theoretical underpinnings of CBT, and its application in clinical practice, the intricate mechanisms through which CBT aids in cognitive restructuring become apparent. By synthesizing research studies on the treatment of various disorders like depression and anxiety, we will uncover the profound impact that challenging and changing negative thought patterns can have on an individual's psychological health and everyday functioning. Ultimately, this essay aims to illuminate the transformative power of CBT in reshaping cognitive processes to promote lasting psychological well-being, while also pointing towards future research avenues and potential applications of CBT in diverse clinical settings.

Overview of CBT

CBT is a widely recognized approach in clinical psychology aimed at changing negative thought patterns. Developed by key figures like Aaron Beck and Albert Ellis, CBT is rooted in the cognitive model of psychopathology, which emphasizes the role of distorted thoughts in emotional disturbances. The basic principles of CBT revolve around the interconnected nature of thoughts, emotions, and behaviors, highlighting how modifying one component can lead to changes in others. Techniques such as cognitive restructuring, problem-solving, and exposure are commonly used in CBT to challenge and reframe negative thinking patterns. Empirical evidence supports the effectiveness of CBT in treating various disorders, particularly in addressing negative thought patterns associated with conditions like depression and anxiety. While CBT has garnered substantial support, criticisms around its efficacy and applicability remain, necessitating further research and exploration of its comparative effectiveness with other therapeutic approaches. By aiding individuals in altering negative thought patterns, CBT plays a crucial role in enhancing psychological well-being and promoting lasting positive change.

Significance in changing negative thought patterns

In altering negative thought patterns, the significance of CBT lies in its fundamental principles and techniques designed to restructure maladaptive cognitions. CBT operates on the premise that our thoughts, emotions, and behaviors are interconnected, influencing one another in a cyclical manner. By identifying irrational or distorted thoughts and challenging them through cognitive restructuring and problem-solving strategies, individuals can effectively modify their negative thought patterns. Through the process of cognitive restructuring, individuals learn to recognize and replace negative thoughts with more rational and positive alternatives, leading to a shift in emotional responses and behavioral patterns. This process not only addresses immediate concerns but also equips individuals with lifelong skills to manage and change negative thought patterns, ultimately promoting psychological well-being and resilience in the face of future challenges.

Thesis statement on the effectiveness of CBT

The effectiveness of CBT in changing negative thought patterns is widely supported by empirical evidence and clinical practice. CBT operates on the premise that individuals' emotions and behaviors are influenced by their thoughts, and by targeting and modifying these negative thought patterns, significant improvements in mental health outcomes can be achieved. Techniques such as cognitive restructuring, problem-solving, and exposure therapy are frequently employed in CBT sessions to challenge and alter maladaptive beliefs and cognitive distortions. By actively engaging patients in these structured exercises, CBT empowers individuals to recognize and change harmful thought patterns, leading to improved mood regulation and behavioral responses. Research studies have consistently demonstrated the efficacy of CBT in treating various mental health disorders, particularly depression and anxiety, by focusing on reshaping negative thought patterns. Despite some criticisms and limitations, the strong empirical support for the effectiveness of CBT in modifying negative thought patterns underscores its vital role in clinical psychology and mental health treatment.

II. HISTORICAL CONTEXT

Founded in the mid-20th century, CBT has emerged as a prominent approach in clinical psychology for modifying negative thought patterns. Rooted in the cognitive model of psychopathology, CBT was pioneered by notable figures like Aaron Beck and Albert Ellis. This therapy emphasizes the interrelation between thoughts, emotions, and behaviors, positing that maladaptive thoughts can lead to psychological distress. By challenging these negative cognitive distortions through structured techniques like cognitive restructuring and problem-solving, CBT aims to alleviate symptoms of various disorders, particularly depression and anxiety. Empirical evidence supports the efficacy of CBT in changing negative thought patterns, showcasing its benefits in improving psychological well-being. However, criticisms have arisen regarding its limitations, necessitating further research to enhance its effectiveness. Understanding the historical context of CBT provides insight into its development and evolution as a leading therapeutic approach in addressing negative thought patterns.

Origins and evolution

The origins and evolution of CBT can be traced back to the pioneering work of Aaron Beck and Albert Ellis in the 1960s. Beck's cognitive therapy and Ellis' rational emotive behavior therapy laid the groundwork for what would become a cornerstone in clinical psychology. CBT is grounded in the cognitive model of psychopathology, emphasizing the interconnectedness of thoughts, emotions, and behaviors. Through cognitive restructuring, problem-solving techniques, and exposure exercises, CBT aims to identify and modify negative thought patterns that contribute to psychological distress. Compared to other therapies like psychodynamic therapy or Acceptance and Commitment Therapy (ACT), CBT offers a structured and goal-oriented approach to empowering individuals to change their cognitive patterns. By harnessing empirical evidence that supports its efficacy in treating various disorders, particularly depression and anxiety, CBT continues to be a leading therapeutic modality in transforming negative thought patterns for improved psychological well-being. With ongoing research and applications, the potential for further advancements in CBT remains promising for the future.

Contributions of Aaron Beck and Albert Ellis

One of the key contributors to the development of CBT as a means to change negative thought patterns was Aaron Beck. Beck's cognitive therapy focused on identifying and altering maladaptive thought patterns, emphasizing the role of cognitive distortions in perpetuating negative emotions and behaviors. Albert Ellis, another pioneering figure in the field, developed Rational Emotive Behavior Therapy (REBT) based on the premise that irrational beliefs underlie psychological distress. Both Beck and Ellis emphasized the importance of challenging and reframing negative thoughts to facilitate behavioral and emotional change. Their approaches have been foundational in shaping CBT, highlighting the interconnectedness of thoughts, emotions, and behaviors in influencing mental health. By integrating cognitive restructuring techniques and challenging irrational beliefs, Beck and Ellis have significantly contributed to the effectiveness of CBT in addressing negative thought patterns and promoting psychological well-being.

The cognitive model of psychopathology

The cognitive model of psychopathology, a fundamental aspect of CBT, posits that negative thought patterns play a pivotal role in the development and maintenance of psychological disorders. Building on the work of key figures like Aaron Beck and Albert Ellis, CBT emphasizes the interconnectedness of thoughts, emotions, and behaviors. Through cognitive restructuring, problem-solving techniques, and exposure exercises, CBT seeks to challenge and modify distorted cognitive processes that contribute to maladaptive behaviors and emotional distress. By targeting these negative thought patterns, CBT aims to instigate lasting changes in individuals' mental health and well-being. Research studies consistently show the efficacy of CBT in treating various disorders, particularly depression and anxiety, by addressing and transforming these negative cognitive patterns. Acknowledging its limitations and criticisms, CBT remains a powerful tool in reshaping individuals' cognitive frameworks for improved psychological functioning.

III. THEORETICAL FOUNDATIONS

The theoretical foundations of CBT are deeply rooted in the cognitive model of psychopathology, which posits that individuals' thoughts, feelings, and behaviors are interconnected. This model, developed by prominent figures like Aaron Beck and Albert Ellis, forms the basis of how CBT aims to change negative thought patterns. By identifying and challenging irrational beliefs, cognitive restructuring helps individuals reframe their negative thinking patterns. Through this process, clients gain insight into the automatic thoughts that drive their emotions and behaviors, enabling them to replace maladaptive cognitions with more adaptive ones. The core principles of CBT emphasize the active role individuals play in shaping their thoughts and reactions, highlighting the empowering nature of this therapeutic approach. Overall, understanding the theoretical underpinnings of CBT provides a solid framework for clinicians to effectively help clients transform their negative thought patterns and improve psychological well-being.

Cognitive theory of emotional response

One of the foundational pillars of CBT lies in the cognitive theory of emotional response, which posits that our emotions are directly influenced by our thoughts and interpretations of events rather than the events themselves. This theory, rooted in the cognitive model of psychopathology, asserts that maladaptive thought patterns contribute to emotional distress and dysfunctional behavior. Through CBT, individuals learn to identify and challenge these negative thought patterns, replacing them with more balanced and rational alternatives. By altering these cognitive distortions, individuals can effectively regulate their emotions and modify their behavior in a more adaptive manner. This cognitive restructuring process serves as a powerful tool in therapy, enabling individuals to not only address their current emotional struggles but also build resilience and coping skills for the future. The application of cognitive theory within CBT underscores the significance of addressing maladaptive cognition in promoting psychological well-being and overall mental health.

The role of maladaptive thoughts in psychopathology

Maladaptive thoughts play a pivotal role in the development and maintenance of psychopathology. These distorted cognitive patterns, such as negative self-perception, catastrophizing, and all-or-nothing thinking, contribute to the reinforcement of maladaptive behaviors and emotions. Drawing from the cognitive model of psychopathology, CBT aims to address these dysfunctional thought processes through cognitive restructuring and challenging irrational beliefs. By targeting these maladaptive thoughts, CBT can effectively modify the individual's behavior and emotions, leading to sustained positive changes in their psychological well-being. Specifically, techniques such as identifying and reframing negative automatic thoughts, reality testing, and behavioral experiments are employed to facilitate this cognitive transformation. Through empirical evidence and clinical application, CBT has been shown to be highly effective in treating various disorders by targeting and altering these maladaptive thought patterns, underscoring its significance in promoting mental health and well-being. Future research should continue to explore the intricate interplay between maladaptive thoughts and psychopathology to further enhance the effectiveness of CBT interventions.

The concept of cognitive distortions

Cognitive distortions, a key concept in CBT, refer to habitual and biased ways of thinking that can lead individuals to perceive reality inaccurately. These distorted thought patterns often fuel negative emotions and behaviors, contributing to the maintenance of psychological distress. By identifying and challenging these cognitive distortions, CBT aims to modify maladaptive thought processes and ultimately alleviate emotional suffering. Through techniques like cognitive restructuring and challenging irrational beliefs, individuals can learn to replace negative distortions with more balanced and realistic thoughts. By addressing the root cause of negative thought patterns, CBT provides a framework for sustainable change and psychological well-being. This therapeutic approach empowers individuals to develop healthier cognitive habits, leading to improved emotional regulation and enhanced overall functioning. Thus, understanding and working to change cognitive distortions are foundational aspects of CBT interventions in clinical practice.

IV. CORE PRINCIPLES

In understanding the core principles of CBT, it becomes apparent that the approach is rooted in the belief that thoughts, emotions, and behaviors are interconnected. CBT operates on the premise that challenging and modifying negative thought patterns can lead to improved emotional well-being and behavioral outcomes. This fundamental principle is applied through techniques like cognitive restructuring, problem-solving, and exposure therapy, which aim to change maladaptive thinking styles. Through the process of identifying and reevaluating distorted beliefs, individuals can gain a more balanced perspective on situations, leading to changes in emotional responses and behaviors. By targeting cognitive distortions and adopting more adaptive ways of thinking, individuals can ultimately break free from negative cycles and cultivate healthier thought patterns, thus enhancing their overall psychological well-being. The efficacy of CBT in changing negative thought patterns is supported by empirical evidence and holds great significance in the field of clinical psychology for its potential to bring about sustainable positive changes in individuals' lives. The future of CBT lies in further research and applications to continue refining its techniques and enhancing its effectiveness in treating a wide range of psychological disorders.

The cognitive-behavioral link

The cognitive-behavioral link in CBT forms the bedrock of its effectiveness in modifying negative thought patterns. This connection between cognitive processes and behavioral responses is central to understanding how individuals interpret and react to life events. By targeting maladaptive thought patterns and behaviors, CBT aims to break the cycle of negative thinking and its accompanying emotional distress. Through techniques like cognitive restructuring and problem-solving, individuals learn to challenge and reframe their negative beliefs, leading to more adaptive behaviors and improved emotional well-being. The interplay between thoughts, emotions, and behaviors is carefully examined in CBT sessions, empowering individuals to identify and change harmful cognitive patterns. This cognitive-behavioral approach serves as a powerful tool for promoting lasting change and enhancing psychological resilience in the face of challenges.

The structured nature

One of the key strengths of CBT lies in its structured nature, which contributes to its effectiveness in changing negative thought patterns. The structured approach of CBT provides a clear framework for both therapists and clients to work through the issues at hand systematically. By breaking down complex problems into smaller, more manageable components, CBT allows individuals to challenge and modify their negative thoughts in a strategic manner. The structured nature of CBT also facilitates the identification of specific cognitive distortions and maladaptive behaviors, leading to targeted interventions that aim to reshape thought patterns. Moreover, this structured approach in CBT ensures consistency and allows for tracking progress over time, enhancing the overall efficacy of the therapy. Ultimately, the structured nature of CBT fosters a collaborative and goal-oriented atmosphere that promotes lasting changes in negative thought patterns.

The goal of cognitive change

CBT aims to facilitate cognitive change by identifying and altering negative thought patterns that contribute to maladaptive behaviors and emotions. At its core, the goal of cognitive change in CBT is to challenge and reframe distorted thinking processes, leading to more adaptive responses and improved mental health outcomes. By working collaboratively with the therapist, individuals learn to recognize, evaluate, and modify their negative automatic thoughts, replacing them with more realistic and balanced perspectives. This process involves examining evidence for and against these thoughts, exploring underlying beliefs and assumptions, and developing coping strategies to effectively manage challenging situations. Through cognitive restructuring techniques and behavioral experiments, individuals can gradually shift their cognitive schemas, leading to sustainable changes in their emotional experiences and behavioral responses. Ultimately, the goal of cognitive change in CBT is to empower individuals to take control of their thought processes and enhance their overall psychological well-being.

V. IDENTIFYING NEGATIVE THOUGHT PATTERNS

Identifying negative thought patterns is a crucial step in the therapeutic process of CBT. By recognizing and understanding these harmful cognitive processes, individuals can begin to challenge and reframe them in a more adaptive manner. One way to identify negative thought patterns is through the process of cognitive restructuring, where individuals learn to identify automatic negative thoughts and examine the evidence that supports or contradicts these beliefs. Additionally, keeping a thought journal can help individuals track their thought patterns throughout the day, providing valuable insights into recurring themes or triggers. By honing in on these negative patterns and understanding their origins, individuals can begin to replace them with more positive and realistic thoughts, ultimately leading to improved emotional well-being and behavioral outcomes. This self-awareness and cognitive shift are at the core of CBT's effectiveness in promoting lasting change.

Recognition of automatic thoughts

In the realm of CBT, the recognition of automatic thoughts plays a crucial role in the process of changing negative thought patterns. Automatic thoughts are the immediate, unfiltered reactions that individuals have in response to situations, often influenced by underlying beliefs. By identifying and challenging these automatic thoughts, individuals undergoing CBT can begin to restructure their cognitive patterns, thus fostering a shift towards more positive and adaptive thought processes. This recognition forms the foundation for cognitive restructuring, a key technique in CBT that involves evaluating the validity and utility of these automatic thoughts. By cultivating an awareness of their automatic thoughts and learning to reframe them in a more rational and constructive manner, individuals can effectively modify their negative thought patterns. Therefore, the acknowledgment and analysis of automatic thoughts serve as a pivotal starting point in the therapeutic journey towards cognitive restructuring and ultimately, improved psychological well-being.

Assessment of thought patterns

Assessment of thought patterns is a fundamental aspect of CBT, where the therapist evaluates the client's cognitive distortions and negative thought patterns. Through various assessment tools and techniques, such as cognitive restructuring exercises or thought diaries, the therapist is able to identify maladaptive thinking patterns that contribute to emotional distress or behavioral issues. By systematically challenging and modifying these thought patterns, individuals can experience significant improvements in their mental health and well-being. This process involves helping the client recognize irrational beliefs, cognitive biases, and automatic negative thoughts, then teaching them alternative, more rational ways of thinking. The thorough assessment of thought patterns in CBT not only aids in addressing immediate symptoms but also equips individuals with skills to manage future challenges more effectively, ultimately leading to lasting positive changes in their mental health.

The impact of negative thoughts on behavior

Negative thoughts have a profound impact on behavior, influencing how individuals perceive, interpret, and respond to various situations. These thoughts can lead to maladaptive behaviors, reinforcing a cycle of negativity and reducing one's overall well-being. CBT aims to address this by challenging and changing these negative thought patterns. By identifying cognitive distortions and irrational beliefs, individuals can learn to reframe their perceptions and adopt more adaptive thinking patterns. As a result, they are better equipped to respond to challenges and stressors in a constructive manner, leading to improved emotional regulation and coping strategies. Through the utilization of techniques such as cognitive restructuring and problem-solving, CBT empowers individuals to take control of their thoughts and behaviors, ultimately fostering resilience and psychological well-being. This therapeutic approach serves as a powerful tool in promoting lasting changes in one's cognitive and behavioral patterns, steering them towards a more positive and fulfilling life.

VI. COGNITIVE RESTRUCTURING

In the realm of CBT, cognitive restructuring stands out as a pivotal technique for modifying negative thought patterns. This process involves identifying and challenging distorted or irrational beliefs that fuel maladaptive behaviors and emotional distress. By encouraging individuals to examine the evidence for and against their negative thoughts, CBT aims to reframe their thinking towards more balanced and constructive perspectives. Through this restructuring, clients can develop greater self-awareness, enhance problem-solving skills, and cultivate a more positive outlook on life. Research has shown that cognitive restructuring is effective in treating various psychological disorders, including depression and anxiety, by addressing the core cognitive distortions that underlie these conditions. By systematically restructuring negative thought patterns, CBT empowers individuals to break free from debilitating cycles of negativity and pave the way for lasting psychological well-being.

Definition and purpose

In the realm of clinical psychology, CBT stands as a formidable tool aimed at reshaping negative thought patterns. Developed by luminaries such as Aaron Beck and Albert Ellis, CBT operates on the premise that thoughts, emotions, and behaviors are intricately interconnected, influencing one another in a cyclical fashion. The primary purpose of CBT is to identify maladaptive thought patterns and replace them with more balanced and constructive ones through techniques like cognitive restructuring and problem-solving. By challenging irrational beliefs and providing patients with practical coping strategies, CBT equips individuals with the tools necessary to navigate challenging circumstances and lead emotionally healthier lives. Through a systematic approach rooted in empirical evidence, CBT showcases its effectiveness in treating various mental health disorders characterized by negative thought patterns, ultimately paving the way towards improved psychological well-being.

Techniques for challenging negative thoughts

One of the key techniques for challenging negative thoughts in CBT is cognitive restructuring. This method involves identifying and challenging irrational or negative beliefs that contribute to distorted thinking patterns. By encouraging individuals to examine the evidence supporting their negative thoughts and consider alternative interpretations, cognitive restructuring aims to replace irrational beliefs with more balanced and realistic ones. Another effective technique is problem-solving, which helps individuals break down overwhelming situations into manageable components and develop practical solutions. Additionally, exposure therapy is used to confront feared situations gradually, allowing individuals to reevaluate their beliefs about the perceived threats. These techniques, when applied in a structured and systematic manner, can help individuals modify maladaptive thought patterns and improve their emotional well-being. Through these strategies, CBT empowers individuals to gain control over their negative thoughts and emotions, enabling them to lead more fulfilling lives.

Case examples of cognitive restructuring

Cognitive restructuring is a fundamental technique in CBT that aims to challenge and modify negative thought patterns. By identifying and replacing irrational or maladaptive thoughts with more rational and positive ones, individuals can effectively change their emotional responses and behaviors. Case examples of cognitive restructuring in CBT illustrate its practical application and transformative impact on individuals experiencing various psychological difficulties. For instance, a case study involving a person with social anxiety disorder may involve challenging thoughts about being judged or rejected in social situations through evidence-based reasoning and alternative perspectives. This process not only helps individuals to alleviate distressing symptoms but also empowers them to develop healthier coping strategies and adaptive behaviors in the long run. Overall, cognitive restructuring demonstrates the powerful influence of changing one's cognitive processes in promoting positive mental health outcomes.

VII. BEHAVIORAL TECHNIQUES

Within the realm of CBT, behavioral techniques play a crucial role in challenging and reshaping negative thought patterns. These techniques involve various strategies aimed at modifying maladaptive behaviors through direct observation, goal setting, and reinforcement. One prominent method is behavioral experiments, where clients test the validity of their negative beliefs in real-life situations. Another effective technique is behavioral activation, which focuses on increasing engagement in positive activities to counteract depressive symptoms. By incorporating these behavioral interventions alongside cognitive restructuring and mindfulness practices, CBT offers a comprehensive approach to transforming negative thought patterns. Through consistent application and therapist guidance, individuals can learn to recognize and modify harmful behaviors, leading to improved emotional well-being and adaptive coping mechanisms. This integration of behavioral techniques within CBT showcases its versatility and efficacy in promoting lasting psychological change.

Behavioral experiments

Behavioral experiments are a fundamental component of CBT aimed at changing negative thought patterns. These experiments involve clients actively testing beliefs or assumptions that contribute to their negative thinking. By challenging these cognitive distortions through real-life experiences, individuals can gather evidence to support more adaptive and realistic thoughts. This process allows clients to recognize the inaccuracies in their previous beliefs and replace them with healthier alternatives. Through structured guidance from the therapist, clients engage in systematic testing of their maladaptive cognitions, fostering insight and promoting cognitive restructuring. By actively participating in these behavioral experiments, individuals can gain a deeper understanding of their thought processes and develop practical strategies to navigate challenging situations. Overall, behavioral experiments serve as a powerful tool in CBT to facilitate lasting changes in cognitive patterns and improve overall psychological well-being.

Exposure therapy

Exposure therapy is a crucial component of CBT when it comes to changing negative thought patterns. By systematically exposing individuals to the feared stimulus or situation, it aims to help them confront and overcome their anxieties or phobias. This process involves a gradual increase in exposure intensity, allowing patients to build tolerance and reduce their avoidance behaviors. Exposure therapy operates on the principle of habituation, wherein repeated exposure under controlled conditions desensitizes individuals to their triggers, leading to a decrease in fear and anxiety responses. This technique challenges maladaptive beliefs by providing tangible evidence that the feared consequences are unlikely to occur, ultimately reshaping negative thought patterns. Through sustained practice and reinforcement, exposure therapy can effectively modify cognitive distortions and foster more adaptive ways of thinking, aiding individuals in overcoming their psychological struggles.

Activity scheduling and behavior activation

Activity scheduling and behavior activation are essential components of CBT when addressing negative thought patterns. By actively engaging individuals in planned, enjoyable activities, therapists can help break the cycle of avoidance and withdrawal commonly associated with depression and anxiety. This process involves identifying activities that bring a sense of accomplishment, pleasure, or mastery to the individual and scheduling them regularly to create a sense of structure and purpose in their lives. Through behavior activation, individuals can experience an increase in positive reinforcements, which then positively impacts their thoughts and emotions. This proactive approach not only helps in gradually changing negative thought patterns but also serves as a stepping stone towards improving overall psychological well-being. By incorporating activity scheduling and behavior activation into CBT sessions, therapists can empower individuals to take control of their lives and break free from the shackles of negative thinking.

VIII. PROBLEM-SOLVING STRATEGIES

Problem-solving strategies play a crucial role in CBT when addressing negative thought patterns. CBT emphasizes the identification of maladaptive thoughts and the implementation of tools to challenge and restructure these patterns effectively. By employing problem-solving techniques, individuals undergoing CBT learn to approach their negative thinking in a systematic and constructive manner. This may involve breaking down complex problems into smaller, more manageable parts, generating alternative solutions, and evaluating the potential outcomes of each option. Clients are encouraged to actively engage in this process, fostering a sense of empowerment and self-efficacy. Through the application of problem-solving strategies in CBT, individuals can develop a more adaptive and resilient mindset, paving the way for lasting changes in their cognitive patterns and emotional well-being.

Teaching problem-solving skills

Teaching problem-solving skills is a crucial component of CBT when addressing negative thought patterns. By equipping individuals with practical problem-solving techniques, therapists enable clients to tackle challenges systematically and rationally. The process often begins with identifying the specific problem, breaking it down into manageable parts, brainstorming potential solutions, evaluating these options, and implementing the best course of action. Through this structured approach, individuals can gain a sense of agency and control over their circumstances, leading to a reduction in negative thinking patterns. By fostering problem-solving skills within the therapeutic setting, clients can learn to navigate everyday dilemmas more effectively, gradually altering their thought processes and emotional responses. This emphasis on problem-solving not only addresses immediate issues but also equips clients with valuable coping strategies that can be applied independently beyond therapy sessions, promoting long-term resilience and psychological well-being.

Application in therapy sessions

In therapy sessions, CBT serves as a powerful tool for altering negative thought patterns. Through a structured approach that targets the interplay between thoughts, emotions, and behaviors, CBT therapists help individuals challenge and reframe their maladaptive cognitions. Techniques like cognitive restructuring, which involves questioning and replacing negative thoughts with more balanced alternatives, are commonly utilized. Additionally, problem-solving skills are honed to reduce the impact of cognitive distortions on emotional well-being. Exposure exercises may also be employed to help individuals confront their fears or anxieties in a controlled and supportive environment. By addressing these negative thought patterns head-on, CBT enables clients to gain a deeper understanding of their thought processes and cultivate more adaptive ways of thinking, ultimately leading to improved mental health outcomes and enhanced coping strategies for the future.

Effectiveness in reducing negative thoughts

When considering the effectiveness of CBT in reducing negative thoughts, it becomes apparent that the structured and goal-oriented nature of CBT plays a significant role. By targeting the cognitive distortions and maladaptive beliefs that underlie negative thought patterns, CBT aims to modify these patterns through cognitive restructuring and evidence-based techniques. The collaborative relationship between the therapist and the client fosters a safe space for exploring and challenging these negative thoughts, ultimately leading to more adaptive and realistic thinking. Research has shown that CBT is highly effective in treating various psychological disorders characterized by negative thought patterns, such as depression and anxiety. By addressing the cognitive components of these conditions, CBT not only reduces symptoms but also provides individuals with the tools to manage and prevent the recurrence of negative thoughts in the future. In conclusion, the efficacy of CBT in changing negative thought patterns underscores its crucial role in promoting psychological well-being and resilience.

IX. THE ROLE OF HOMEWORK

Homework assignments play a crucial role in CBT by extending therapeutic interventions beyond the clinical sessions. Through homework, individuals are encouraged to practice and apply the cognitive restructuring techniques learned in therapy to real-life situations. This process allows for the reinforcement of new adaptive thought patterns and behaviors while challenging and modifying negative cognitive distortions ingrained over time. Engaging in homework assignments also fosters empowerment and self-efficacy, as clients actively participate in their own therapeutic progress. By consistently practicing new cognitive strategies outside of therapy sessions, individuals can generalize these skills to various contexts, leading to lasting changes in their thought processes and emotional responses. Ultimately, the integration of homework assignments enhances the effectiveness of CBT in facilitating enduring transformations in negative thought patterns and improving overall psychological well-being.

Purpose and types of homework assignments

The purpose and types of homework assignments in CBT play a crucial role in reinforcing and extending the therapeutic process beyond the clinical setting. Homework assignments serve to consolidate learning, practice new skills, and challenge negative thought patterns outside of therapy sessions. These tasks can vary in nature, including thought records, behavioral experiments, relaxation exercises, or exposure tasks, tailored to each individual's unique needs and treatment goals. By engaging in homework assignments, clients actively participate in their own therapeutic journey, fostering self-awareness and empowerment in the process of changing negative thought patterns. Effective homework assignments are structured, specific, and collaborative between the therapist and client, ensuring relevance and feasibility. Ultimately, these tasks serve as a bridge between therapy sessions, promoting continuity and long-term change in cognitive patterns and behaviors.

Compliance and its impact on therapy outcomes

Compliance, or the patient's commitment to engaging in therapy and following the prescribed interventions, plays a crucial role in determining the efficacy of CBT in changing negative thought patterns. The impact of compliance on therapy outcomes cannot be overstated, as a lack of adherence to CBT techniques can hinder progress and diminish the potential benefits of treatment. When clients fully engage with the cognitive restructuring exercises, homework assignments, and behavioral experiments recommended by their therapist, they are more likely to experience significant improvements in their thought patterns and overall psychological well-being. Therefore, therapists must not only deliver effective interventions but also foster a strong therapeutic alliance to enhance compliance and ensure positive outcomes in CBT. By acknowledging the importance of compliance and actively working to promote it, therapists can maximize the potential of CBT in facilitating lasting changes in negative cognitive patterns.

Strategies to enhance homework adherence

In considering strategies to enhance homework adherence within the framework of CBT, it is crucial to acknowledge the importance of fostering a collaborative and empathetic therapeutic relationship between the therapist and client. This alliance serves as the foundation for promoting client motivation and commitment to completing assigned homework tasks, which are integral to achieving successful outcomes in CBT. The therapist can enhance homework adherence by collaboratively setting realistic and achievable goals, individualizing assignments to the client's specific needs and preferences, and providing regular feedback and support to address any challenges that may arise. Furthermore, incorporating motivational interviewing techniques and behavioral activation strategies can further promote engagement and persistence in completing homework tasks. By employing these tailored strategies, therapists can optimize the effectiveness of CBT interventions and facilitate meaningful changes in negative thought patterns that underlie various psychological disorders.

X. THE THERAPEUTIC RELATIONSHIP

In CBT, the therapeutic relationship plays a crucial role in facilitating the change of negative thought patterns. The foundation of CBT lies in the collaborative partnership between the therapist and the client, where mutual respect, trust, and empathy are essential components. Through this relationship, the therapist creates a safe and supportive environment for the client to explore their thoughts, emotions, and behaviors. By actively listening, providing feedback, and offering guidance, the therapist helps the client challenge and reframe their maladaptive cognitive distortions. Additionally, the therapeutic relationship fosters a sense of empowerment and self-efficacy in the client, as they learn to take control of their thoughts and behaviors. Ultimately, a strong therapeutic relationship in CBT serves as the catalyst for meaningful and lasting changes in the client's cognitive processes, leading to improved psychological well-being and quality of life.

Collaboration between therapist and client

Collaboration between the therapist and the client is essential in the successful application of CBT to change negative thought patterns. Establishing a strong therapeutic alliance at the outset creates a safe space for the client to explore their thoughts and emotions openly. By working collaboratively, the therapist can guide the client in identifying these negative thought patterns and understanding their influence on emotions and behaviors. Through mutual effort, the therapist can introduce various CBT techniques like cognitive restructuring or problem-solving to challenge and reframe these patterns effectively. A supportive and trusting relationship allows the client to actively engage in the therapeutic process, leading to more significant changes in their cognitive distortions. Effective collaboration ensures that the client feels empowered and invested in their own mental health journey, ultimately resulting in more positive outcomes.

The role of therapist's attitudes and behaviors

In cognitive-behavioral therapy, the role of the therapist's attitudes and behaviors is paramount in facilitating the change of negative thought patterns in clients. A therapist's positive regard, empathy, and genuineness are essential in creating a therapeutic alliance where the client feels safe to explore their thoughts and emotions. Furthermore, the therapist's ability to challenge negative beliefs, provide cognitive restructuring techniques, and offer alternative perspectives plays a vital role in guiding the client towards more adaptive thought patterns. By modeling problem-solving skills and demonstrating a non-judgmental attitude, therapists can empower clients to challenge their negative thoughts and behaviors effectively. Ultimately, the therapist's attitudes and behaviors serve as a catalyst for changing negative thought patterns, fostering a constructive and collaborative therapeutic environment conducive to cognitive restructuring and emotional growth in clients.

Building trust and rapport

Building trust and rapport are fundamental components of effective CBT when aiming to change negative thought patterns. Establishing a strong therapeutic alliance is essential for fostering collaboration between the therapist and the client, enhancing treatment outcomes. At the beginning of therapy, trust serves as the foundation upon which the therapeutic relationship is built. It allows the client to feel safe, understood, and valued, creating an environment where they can explore and challenge their negative thought patterns without fear of judgment. Throughout the therapy process, maintaining rapport through empathy, active listening, and genuine interest in the client's experiences further solidifies the trust established initially. This bond enables the therapist to effectively introduce and implement cognitive restructuring techniques, challenge distorted beliefs, and guide the client towards adopting healthier thought patterns. Ultimately, building trust and rapport in CBT is integral to facilitating meaningful and lasting changes in the client's cognitive processes and promoting psychological well-being.

XI. DEPRESSION

CBT for depression is a widely studied and effective treatment approach. By targeting negative thought patterns, CBT aims to challenge and reframe distorted beliefs that contribute to depressive symptoms. Patients are guided to identify automatic negative thoughts, examine the evidence supporting these thoughts, and develop more balanced and realistic perspectives. Through cognitive restructuring techniques, individuals are encouraged to replace maladaptive thoughts with more positive and adaptive alternatives. Behavioral activation strategies are also employed to encourage individuals to engage in activities that bring them a sense of pleasure and accomplishment, combating the lethargy often associated with depression. Research has consistently shown CBT to be effective in reducing depressive symptoms and preventing relapse, making it a first-line treatment for depression. However, further research is needed to explore the long-term effectiveness and mechanisms of change in CBT for depression.

Prevalence and impact of depression

Depression is a pervasive mental health issue globally, affecting millions of individuals across various age groups and demographics. The prevalence of depression underscores its significant impact on individuals, families, and communities, leading to impaired functioning and reduced quality of life. Research has shown that individuals struggling with depression often experience negative thought patterns, such as cognitive distortions and self-critical beliefs, exacerbating their emotional distress. These negative thought patterns can perpetuate the cycle of depression, making it challenging for individuals to break free from its grip. CBT stands out as an effective intervention in addressing these negative thought patterns by identifying and challenging maladaptive cognitions. By modifying these distorted thoughts and promoting more adaptive thinking styles, CBT equips individuals with the necessary tools to combat depression and improve overall psychological well-being. The widespread prevalence of depression and its detrimental impact underscore the importance of interventions like CBT in facilitating positive change in individuals' mental health.

CBT interventions for depressive thoughts

In addressing depressive thoughts using CBT interventions, one primary method is cognitive restructuring. By identifying and challenging negative automatic thoughts, individuals can learn to replace them with more balanced and positive alternatives. This process involves recognizing distorted thinking patterns, such as all-or-nothing thinking or catastrophizing, and working to develop a more accurate and helpful perspective. Additionally, problem-solving techniques can be employed to address specific issues contributing to depressive thoughts, enabling individuals to develop practical strategies for managing challenges more effectively. Exposure techniques may also be utilized to gradually confront feared situations or triggers, helping individuals to reevaluate their fears and reduce avoidance behaviors. Through a combination of these methods, CBT can effectively target and modify the cognitive processes underlying depressive thoughts, leading to meaningful improvements in mood and overall well-being.

Outcome studies and effectiveness

Outcome studies and effectiveness are vital components in evaluating the success of CBT in changing negative thought patterns. Numerous research studies have demonstrated the efficacy of CBT in treating various mental health disorders, particularly depression and anxiety. These outcome studies often use standardized measures to quantify improvements in cognitive distortions, maladaptive beliefs, and emotional regulation. By analyzing pre- and post-treatment data, researchers can evaluate the effectiveness of CBT interventions in modifying negative thought patterns and improving overall psychological well-being. However, some critics argue that outcome studies may not capture the full complexity of human experience or the long-term effects of treatment. Therefore, future research should aim to incorporate more qualitative measures to provide a holistic understanding of how CBT facilitates lasting changes in individuals' cognitive processes and emotional responses.

XII. ANXIETY DISORDERS

CBT has proven to be particularly effective in treating anxiety disorders by targeting and modifying negative thought patterns. By addressing the cognitive distortions and maladaptive beliefs underlying anxiety, CBT aims to restructure these patterns to alleviate symptoms and improve overall well-being. The core principles of CBT, centered around the interplay between thoughts, emotions, and behaviors, provide a framework for identifying and challenging irrational thoughts that fuel anxiety. Techniques such as cognitive restructuring, problem-solving strategies, and exposure therapy are frequently employed to facilitate this process. Research studies have consistently demonstrated the efficacy of CBT in reducing anxiety symptoms and preventing relapse, underscoring its role as a gold standard treatment. Despite its success, ongoing research is needed to further refine and expand the application of CBT for various anxiety disorders, ensuring continued advancements in clinical practice and enhancing outcomes for individuals struggling with anxiety.

Understanding anxiety through the CBT lens

In the realm of clinical psychology, CBT stands out as a widely utilized approach to address and modify negative thought patterns. By delving into the intricate interplay between thoughts, emotions, and behaviors, CBT offers a holistic framework for understanding anxiety through a cognitive lens. Rooted in the cognitive model of psychopathology, CBT targets maladaptive beliefs and automatic thoughts that perpetuate anxiety. Through techniques like cognitive restructuring, individuals learn to challenge and reframe their negative thought patterns, ultimately fostering a shift towards more adaptive cognitions. By systematically addressing these cognitive distortions, CBT equips individuals with the tools to navigate anxious feelings more effectively. A thorough examination of anxiety through the CBT lens unveils the nuanced processes involved in identifying and altering negative thought patterns, ultimately paving the way for enhanced psychological well-being.

Tailoring CBT for different anxiety disorders

Tailoring CBT to address different anxiety disorders is crucial for effective treatment outcomes. Each anxiety disorder, whether it be generalized anxiety disorder, social anxiety disorder, panic disorder, or specific phobias, presents unique cognitive distortions and behavioral patterns that need to be targeted specifically. A tailored approach involves identifying the predominant negative thought patterns and maladaptive behaviors characteristic of each disorder and then utilizing specialized techniques within the framework of CBT to address these issues. For instance, exposure therapy may be particularly beneficial for individuals with specific phobias, while cognitive restructuring techniques might be more effective for those with generalized anxiety disorder. By customizing CBT interventions to suit the specific needs of individuals with different anxiety disorders, clinicians can optimize treatment efficacy and ultimately help clients achieve long-lasting relief from their symptoms.

Review of treatment outcomes

With regards to the review of treatment outcomes in CBT for changing negative thought patterns, empirical evidence consistently supports its efficacy in addressing a range of psychological disorders. Research studies have demonstrated significant improvements in symptoms of depression, anxiety, and other mental health issues following CBT interventions. By targeting the core cognitive distortions and maladaptive thought patterns, CBT seeks to bring about lasting changes in how individuals perceive and interpret their experiences. This approach is supported by the cognitive model of psychopathology, which highlights the role of cognitive processes in shaping emotional and behavioral responses. Despite some criticisms and limitations, such as the brief nature of some CBT interventions and the challenges in assessing long-term outcomes, CBT remains a widely utilized and effective therapeutic approach for modifying negative thought patterns and improving overall psychological well-being. Further research is needed to explore the mechanisms underlying these treatment outcomes and to refine the techniques used in CBT practice.

XIII. OTHER PSYCHOLOGICAL DISORDERS

While CBT is commonly associated with treating anxiety and depression, its application extends to various other psychological disorders. By targeting dysfunctional thought patterns and behaviors, CBT has shown efficacy in addressing conditions such as obsessive-compulsive disorder, post-traumatic stress disorder, eating disorders, and bipolar disorder. In these cases, CBT aims to challenge maladaptive beliefs, coping strategies, and behavioral responses unique to each disorder. For instance, in OCD, CBT may involve exposure and response prevention to reduce compulsive behaviors. Similarly, in eating disorders, cognitive restructuring is used to address distorted body image perceptions. The adaptability of CBT to diverse psychological conditions underscores its versatility and effectiveness in facilitating cognitive and behavioral change beyond anxiety and depression, ultimately enhancing overall psychological well-being. Future research could further explore the nuances of CBT applications across various disorders to optimize treatment outcomes.

Application to a range of disorders

Application of CBT to a range of disorders showcases its versatility and efficacy in clinical practice. By targeting negative thought patterns, CBT can be effectively applied to conditions such as depression, anxiety, OCD, PTSD, and eating disorders. Through cognitive restructuring, individuals learn to identify and challenge maladaptive beliefs, leading to improved emotional regulation and behavioral responses. CBT also employs techniques like problem-solving and exposure therapy to confront and modify negative thought patterns in a systematic manner. The empirical evidence supporting the success of CBT in treating various disorders is robust, emphasizing its ability to facilitate lasting change in individuals' cognitive processes. By addressing negative thought patterns at their core, CBT offers a powerful tool for promoting psychological well-being and enhancing overall quality of life. Further research and exploration of CBT applications in diverse populations and settings hold promise for advancing mental health interventions.

Modifications to the CBT approach

Modifications to the CBT approach have been a subject of ongoing study and debate within the field of clinical psychology. While the traditional CBT model focuses on identifying and challenging negative thought patterns through cognitive restructuring and behavioral techniques, recent developments have seen a shift towards more tailored and nuanced interventions. One such modification involves incorporating mindfulness-based practices to enhance awareness and acceptance of negative thoughts without judgment. This addition aligns CBT with principles of mindfulness-based therapies, aiming to promote greater emotional regulation and resilience. Additionally, the integration of positive psychology principles, emphasizing strengths and virtues, has been shown to complement traditional CBT strategies, fostering a more holistic approach to addressing negative thought patterns. These modifications represent an evolution in the CBT framework, offering new avenues for effectively addressing cognitive distortions and improving overall mental well-being. Further research and exploration of these adaptations hold promise for expanding the efficacy and reach of CBT in clinical practice.

Evidence of effectiveness across disorders

Evidence of CBT's effectiveness across various disorders is well-documented, highlighting its versatility in addressing negative thought patterns. Studies on depression, anxiety, and post-traumatic stress disorder consistently show significant improvements in symptoms post-CBT intervention. For instance, in the treatment of depression, CBT has been found to be as effective as pharmacotherapy and may even provide longer-lasting benefits. Furthermore, CBT's adaptability allows for tailored interventions based on individual needs, making it a personalized and efficient therapeutic approach. This evidence underscores the importance of CBT in not only changing negative thought patterns but also in treating the underlying psychological conditions. However, despite these positive findings, some criticisms of CBT exist, such as its limited focus on unconscious processes. Overall, the empirical evidence supports CBT as a valuable tool in altering negative thought patterns and promoting mental well-being across diverse populations.

XIV. GROUP SETTINGS

When considering the application of CBT in group settings, various factors need to be taken into account for its effectiveness. While individual therapy sessions offer personalized attention to specific needs, group therapy provides a unique opportunity for interpersonal learning and support. In a group setting, individuals can observe and learn from the experiences and coping strategies of others, which can be particularly beneficial in changing negative thought patterns. Additionally, group therapy sessions create a sense of community and shared understanding, reducing feelings of isolation commonly associated with negative thinking. However, challenges may arise in managing diverse group dynamics and ensuring that all participants receive adequate attention and support. Despite these challenges, CBT in group settings proves to be a valuable tool in promoting cognitive restructuring and behavioral change among individuals struggling with negative thought patterns.

Advantages of group therapy

Group therapy offers several advantages in the context of CBT for changing negative thought patterns. Firstly, the group dynamic allows individuals to gain insight from the experiences and perspectives of others facing similar challenges, fostering a sense of universality and reducing feelings of isolation. This mutual support and shared understanding can be empowering, leading to increased motivation and commitment to the therapeutic process. Additionally, group therapy provides a platform for practicing social skills and receiving feedback in a safe environment, aiding in the development of healthier interpersonal relationships. Moreover, the diverse array of personalities within the group can challenge rigid thought patterns and encourage alternative perspectives, promoting cognitive flexibility and resilience in the face of adversity. Overall, the communal nature of group therapy in CBT can enhance the efficacy of interventions aimed at restructuring negative thought patterns by leveraging the power of collective insight and support.

Dynamics and outcomes of group CBT

Group CBT has been shown to be an effective intervention for individuals struggling with negative thought patterns. The dynamic nature of group therapy allows participants to engage with others who share similar cognitive distortions, providing a sense of validation and support. Through group discussions and activities, individuals can challenge their negative beliefs and gain new perspectives on their thought patterns. The collective experience fosters a sense of community and encourages participants to hold each other accountable for implementing coping strategies learned in therapy. Group CBT also offers a platform for social learning and skill development, as individuals observe and model adaptive behaviors from their peers. The outcomes of group CBT often include improved self-awareness, enhanced coping skills, and a reduction in negative thinking patterns, highlighting the value of this therapeutic approach in promoting positive change within a supportive peer environment.

Managing group processes and negative thoughts

When managing group processes in CBT, it is crucial to address negative thoughts that may arise within the group dynamiNegative thoughts can hinder the progress of therapy and perpetuate unhelpful behaviors and emotions. By actively managing these negative thoughts, therapists can create a more positive and productive group environment, ultimately promoting better outcomes for all participants. This can be achieved through techniques such as cognitive restructuring, where individuals are encouraged to challenge and replace their negative thoughts with more realistic and adaptive ones. Additionally, group members may benefit from problem-solving strategies to address their specific concerns and fears. By actively engaging with and changing negative thought patterns within the group setting, therapists can facilitate a more collaborative and supportive atmosphere, enhancing the overall effectiveness of CBT interventions.

XV. CHILDREN AND ADOLESCENTS

In the realm of CBT, the application of this therapeutic approach with children and adolescents warrants special consideration. This population presents unique challenges and opportunities due to their developing cognitive capacities and emotional experiences. When working with children and adolescents, therapists must adapt CBT techniques to suit their developmental stage and individual needs. Strategies such as cognitive restructuring may need to be simplified or supplemented with creative interventions like play therapy or art therapy to enhance engagement and understanding. Additionally, building rapport and establishing trust are crucial components of effective therapy with young clients. By tailoring CBT to meet the specific developmental needs of children and adolescents, therapists can effectively intervene in negative thought patterns early on, paving the way for healthier cognitive and emotional functioning in adulthood.

Adapting CBT for younger populations

Adapting CBT for younger populations is crucial for effective intervention in childhood and adolescent mental health. By recognizing the unique developmental needs and cognitive capacities of children and teenagers, therapists can tailor CBT techniques to be more engaging and accessible. Incorporating age-appropriate language, creative visualization, and playful activities can enhance the effectiveness of CBT in younger individuals. Additionally, involving parents or caregivers in therapy sessions can provide additional support and reinforce positive changes in the child's thought patterns and behaviors. However, it is essential to carefully adapt CBT strategies to suit the developmental stage and specific needs of each young client to maximize therapeutic outcomes. Ultimately, by customizing CBT for younger populations, mental health professionals can promote long-lasting positive changes in negative thought patterns, paving the way for healthier emotional development and improved overall well-being in children and adolescents.

Techniques for engaging children and teens

Techniques for engaging children and teens in CBT are crucial for effective outcomes. One approach involves using creative and age-appropriate activities to help them understand and challenge their negative thought patterns. For children, using games, drawing, or storytelling can make the therapeutic process more engaging and less intimidating. Teens may respond well to journaling, role-playing, or guided imagery exercises to explore and reframe their negative beliefs. Establishing a trusting and supportive therapeutic relationship is also vital, as it encourages open communication and collaboration in addressing cognitive distortions. By tailoring CBT techniques to suit the developmental stages and interests of children and teens, therapists can effectively address negative thought patterns and facilitate lasting change in their mental health and well-being. These methods not only empower young individuals to overcome their challenges but also equip them with valuable coping skills for the future.

Efficacy of CBT in youth

CBT has been widely recognized for its efficacy in changing negative thought patterns, especially in youth. By targeting the cognitive distortions and maladaptive beliefs that underlie these negative thoughts, CBT helps individuals develop healthier thinking patterns and coping strategies. In youth, CBT has shown promising results in treating various psychological disorders, including anxiety, depression, and behavioral problems. It equips young individuals with the skills to challenge and reframe their negative thoughts, leading to improved emotional regulation and increased resilience. Research studies have consistently demonstrated the effectiveness of CBT in youth populations, showcasing long-lasting benefits beyond the therapy sessions. While limitations and criticisms exist, the empirical evidence overwhelmingly supports the use of CBT as a valuable intervention for changing negative thought patterns in youth, ultimately contributing to their overall psychological well-being and quality of life.

XVI. DIVERSE POPULATIONS

In the realm of CBT, the application of its principles to diverse populations is paramount in ensuring effective treatment outcomes. As individuals from various cultural backgrounds may exhibit unique belief systems and thought patterns, therapists must tailor their approach to address the specific needs of each group. By acknowledging and respecting cultural nuances, therapists can establish a rapport with clients that facilitates the modification of negative thought patterns. Moreover, adapting CBT techniques to align with diverse populations requires a deep understanding of how societal influences impact cognitive processes. By integrating cultural sensitivity into the therapeutic process, CBT can effectively assist individuals in challenging their maladaptive beliefs and behaviors, ultimately promoting positive change and psychological well-being across diverse populations. This intersection of CBT and cultural diversity underscores the importance of a nuanced and inclusive approach to therapy.

Cultural considerations in CBT

Cultural considerations play a crucial role in the effectiveness of CBT in modifying negative thought patterns. These considerations involve understanding the client's cultural background, beliefs, values, and traditions that may influence their cognitive processes and interpretations of events. Culturally sensitive therapists need to tailor CBT interventions to align with the client's cultural norms and preferences, ensuring the therapy is relevant and engaging for the individual. By integrating cultural factors into the therapeutic process, therapists can promote a deeper level of understanding and rapport with their clients, leading to more successful outcomes in changing negative thought patterns. Moreover, addressing cultural considerations in CBT helps to avoid potential misunderstandings or conflicts that may arise due to differences in cultural perspectives, ultimately enhancing the overall effectiveness and applicability of CBT across diverse populations.

Tailoring CBT to diverse client needs

Tailoring CBT to diverse client needs is essential in ensuring the efficacy of this therapeutic approach. While the fundamental principles of CBT encompass identifying, challenging, and modifying negative thought patterns, the application of these principles must be customized to accommodate the unique characteristics and experiences of each individual. This customization involves recognizing cultural differences, personal beliefs, and past traumas that may influence the way clients perceive and interpret their thoughts. By acknowledging these factors, therapists can adapt CBT techniques, such as cognitive restructuring and problem-solving, to suit clients' specific needs. Additionally, incorporating components of other therapeutic modalities, such as mindfulness or narrative therapy, can further enhance the effectiveness of CBT in addressing diverse client populations. Ultimately, tailoring CBT to individual clients not only increases treatment outcomes but also fosters a more inclusive and person-centered approach to mental health care.

Research on CBT across cultures

Research on CBT across cultures has shown promising results in addressing negative thought patterns. While traditional CBT techniques have been primarily developed in Western contexts, there is a growing body of literature that examines its effectiveness in diverse cultural settings. Studies have found that CBT can be adapted to suit the values, beliefs, and norms of different cultures, making it a universally applicable therapeutic approach. By incorporating cultural factors into the therapy process, such as language, communication styles, and cultural narratives, CBT can effectively help individuals from various backgrounds challenge and reframe negative thought patterns. This cross-cultural application of CBT highlights the flexibility and relevance of this therapeutic approach in promoting mental well-being across different societies. Further research in this area can continue to enrich our understanding of how CBT can be tailored to meet the needs of diverse populations, contributing to the global dissemination of effective mental health interventions.

XVII. TECHNOLOGICAL ADVANCES

The field of CBT has seen significant advancements due to technology. The integration of technology into CBT has opened up new avenues for treatment delivery and accessibility. Web-based CBT programs, mobile applications, and virtual reality platforms have been developed to enhance the efficacy of traditional CBT interventions. These technological tools allow individuals to access therapy remotely, receive personalized feedback, and engage in interactive exercises to challenge and modify negative thought patterns. Moreover, virtual reality exposure therapy has revolutionized the treatment of anxiety disorders by providing a safe and controlled environment for facing feared stimuli. These technological advances not only increase the reach of CBT but also improve treatment outcomes by offering novel ways to deliver evidence-based interventions. As technology continues to evolve, the integration of innovative tools into CBT holds promise for further enhancing therapeutic effectiveness and ultimately improving mental health outcomes.

Online CBT programs and their efficacy

Online CBT programs have garnered increasing attention for their potential efficacy in addressing negative thought patterns. These programs offer individuals the opportunity to engage in therapeutic interventions from the comfort of their own homes, making mental health support more accessible and convenient. By leveraging the principles of CBT, these online programs can help individuals identify and challenge maladaptive thought patterns that contribute to psychological distress. Through techniques such as cognitive restructuring and problem-solving, clients can learn to reframe negative thoughts and develop healthier cognitive habits. While empirical evidence supporting the effectiveness of online CBT programs is emerging, there are still concerns regarding the quality of therapeutic relationships and the level of personalized care compared to traditional face-to-face therapy. Future research should continue to explore the nuances of online CBT interventions to optimize their efficacy in promoting lasting changes in negative thought patterns and overall psychological well-being.

Use of mobile apps in CBT

The use of mobile applications in CBT has gained significant traction in recent years, offering a convenient and accessible platform for individuals seeking therapeutic support. These apps often provide features such as mood tracking, cognitive restructuring exercises, and guided relaxation techniques, allowing users to engage in CBT principles in their daily lives. By incorporating technology into therapy, individuals can receive timely support and interventions when faced with negative thought patterns or challenging emotional states. However, while mobile apps can enhance the reach and efficiency of CBT, it is crucial to consider the quality and credibility of these applications, as well as the potential limitations in providing personalized treatment. Further research is needed to evaluate the effectiveness of mobile apps in delivering CBT and their impact on long-term outcomes for individuals struggling with negative thought patterns.

Virtual reality and its application in CBT

Virtual Reality (VR) technology has emerged as a novel tool in the realm of CBT, offering unique opportunities to address negative thought patterns in a more immersive and engaging manner. By simulating real-world scenarios within a controlled environment, VR allows individuals to confront and challenge their maladaptive beliefs and behaviors in a safe yet realistic setting. These virtual environments can be tailored to specific phobias, anxieties, or traumas, providing a targeted approach to cognitive restructuring and exposure therapy. Research has shown promising results in utilizing VR interventions for various mental health conditions, showcasing its potential to enhance the efficacy of traditional CBT techniques. As the field continues to evolve, exploring the integration of VR in CBT holds promise for revolutionizing therapeutic approaches and promoting lasting change in individuals' cognitive processes and emotional well-being.

XVIII. INTEGRATION OF MINDFULNESS

The integration of mindfulness practices in CBT has gained increasing attention in recent years due to its potential to enhance the effectiveness of traditional CBT techniques. Mindfulness, rooted in Eastern traditions, emphasizes focused awareness of the present moment without judgment. When integrated into CBT, mindfulness can help individuals develop a greater awareness of their negative thought patterns, allowing them to more effectively challenge and reframe these thoughts. By incorporating mindfulness techniques such as meditation and body scans, CBT therapists can assist clients in developing a deeper understanding of the connection between their thoughts, emotions, and behaviors. This integrative approach can lead to a more holistic therapeutic experience, promoting long-term positive changes in thought processes and overall psychological well-being. Further research in this area is warranted to explore the full potential of integrating mindfulness into CBT practice.

Mindfulness-Based Cognitive Therapy (MBCT)

MBCT serves as an innovative approach within the realm of CBT, focusing on integrating mindfulness techniques with cognitive restructuring to target negative thought patterns. At its core, MBCT aims to cultivate non-judgmental awareness of one's thoughts and feelings, particularly those associated with depression and anxiety. By fostering mindfulness, individuals can develop the ability to observe their negative thoughts without becoming entangled in them, leading to greater emotional regulation and reduced reactivity. Through this process, individuals can effectively challenge and reframe their negative cognitive patterns, ultimately promoting psychological well-being and resilience. Research has shown that MBCT can be particularly effective in preventing relapse in individuals with recurrent depression, highlighting its value in addressing chronic negative thought patterns. By incorporating mindfulness practices into traditional CBT, MBCT offers a comprehensive and holistic approach to changing negative thought patterns and promoting mental health.

The role of mindfulness in managing thoughts

One crucial aspect in managing negative thought patterns within the realm of CBT is the role of mindfulness. Mindfulness, a practice rooted in Buddhist tradition and popularized in contemporary psychology, involves cultivating present moment awareness without judgment. By incorporating mindfulness techniques into CBT, individuals can develop greater insight into their thought processes and emotional reactions, creating distance from negative thoughts and enhancing the ability to respond rather than react impulsively. Through mindfulness, individuals can observe their thoughts more objectively, recognizing them as passing mental events rather than absolute truths. This shift in perspective enables individuals to challenge and reframe negative narrative patterns more effectively, ultimately fostering healthier cognitive patterns and emotional responses. By actively integrating mindfulness practices into CBT interventions, individuals can gain greater control over their thoughts and emotions, leading to lasting changes in their overall well-being.

Comparative studies on MBCT and traditional CBT

Comparative studies on MBCT and traditional CBT have garnered significant attention in recent years. While both approaches aim to address negative thought patterns, they differ in their underlying mechanisms and techniques. MBCT integrates elements of mindfulness practices with cognitive therapy, emphasizing acceptance and present moment awareness to help individuals manage negative thoughts and emotions. In contrast, traditional CBT primarily focuses on identifying and challenging maladaptive thoughts through cognitive restructuring and behavior modification. Research suggests that MBCT may be more effective in preventing relapse in individuals with recurrent depression, while traditional CBT shows efficacy in treating a broader range of psychological conditions. Future comparative studies should delve deeper into the specific mechanisms of change in each approach to better inform therapeutic interventions and maximize outcomes for individuals struggling with negative thought patterns.

XIX. THE ROLE OF EMOTIONS

Emotions play a crucial role in CBT as they are closely intertwined with thoughts and behaviors. In CBT, negative emotional responses are often linked to maladaptive thought patterns, contributing to conditions such as depression and anxiety. By addressing these negative emotions through cognitive restructuring and behavioral interventions, CBT aims to modify dysfunctional thought patterns effectively. Therapists help individuals identify the underlying emotions associated with their negative thoughts and work towards changing these patterns to foster more adaptive responses. This process involves exploring the connections between thoughts, emotions, and behaviors to develop healthier coping strategies and promote positive emotional regulation. By acknowledging the significance of emotions in CBT, therapists can guide individuals towards a more balanced and constructive mental outlook, ultimately leading to improved psychological well-being and resilience.

Emotional regulation strategies

Emotional regulation strategies play a pivotal role in CBT when addressing negative thought patterns. Through the process of cognitive restructuring, individuals are encouraged to identify and challenge distorted and unhelpful thoughts, replacing them with more rational and balanced ones. Moreover, techniques such as problem-solving and exposure therapy are utilized to help individuals confront their fears and negative beliefs in a gradual and controlled manner. By actively engaging with these strategies, individuals can develop a greater sense of self-awareness and emotional control, leading to improved mental health outcomes. The integration of these emotional regulation strategies into CBT not only empowers individuals to overcome negative thought patterns but also equips them with lifelong tools for managing their emotions effectively. Thus, these strategies form a fundamental component of the therapeutic process, facilitating profound cognitive shifts that promote lasting positive change.

Addressing emotional reasoning

Addressing emotional reasoning in CBT is crucial for modifying negative thought patterns. Emotional reasoning is a cognitive distortion where individuals believe that their emotions reflect objective reality, leading to biased perceptions and interpretations. In the context of CBT, challenging emotional reasoning involves helping clients recognize that feelings are not always accurate reflections of reality, and that they can be influenced by thoughts and beliefs. By encouraging clients to examine evidence for and against their negative thoughts, therapists can assist in restructuring cognitive distortions and promoting more realistic, balanced thinking. This process not only helps individuals develop healthier thought patterns but also fosters emotional regulation and resilience. Ultimately, addressing emotional reasoning in CBT plays a vital role in improving psychological well-being and overall functioning.

The interplay between thoughts and emotions

In the realm of CBT, the interplay between thoughts and emotions holds significant importance in understanding and transforming negative thought patterns. At the core of this therapeutic approach lies the recognition that thoughts influence emotions, and vice versa, creating a cyclical relationship that can either perpetuate or alleviate distress. By identifying and challenging maladaptive thoughts, individuals undergoing CBT can disrupt this cycle, leading to a shift in emotional responses and subsequent behaviors. This process involves unpacking cognitive distortions, such as black-and-white thinking or catastrophizing, and replacing them with more balanced and rational alternatives. Through techniques like cognitive restructuring and behavioral experiments, individuals can not only modify their negative thought patterns but also cultivate resilience and self-awareness in navigating life's challenges. Ultimately, this intricate dance between thoughts and emotions in CBT offers a transformative pathway towards healing and psychological well-being.

XX. THE IMPACT ON SELF-ESTEEM

CBT has shown significant impact on self-esteem by targeting negative thought patterns that can perpetuate low self-worth. Through cognitive restructuring techniques, individuals are guided to challenge and reframe their negative beliefs about themselves, thus promoting a more positive self-perception. By addressing distorted thinking patterns and replacing them with more adaptive cognitions, CBT helps individuals develop a healthier mindset that fosters self-acceptance and self-confidence. Additionally, CBT equips individuals with practical strategies to cope with setbacks and failures, enhancing their resilience and overall sense of self-efficacy. Research studies have consistently indicated the effectiveness of CBT in improving self-esteem, particularly in individuals struggling with conditions like depression and anxiety. Therefore, the integration of CBT into therapeutic interventions not only alleviates psychological distress but also cultivates a more positive self-image, ultimately contributing to enhanced psychological well-being.

CBT interventions targeting self-worth

In the realm of CBT, interventions targeting self-worth play a pivotal role in reshaping negative thought patterns. CBT, known for its evidence-based approach in addressing psychological difficulties, emphasizes the interconnectedness between thoughts, emotions, and behaviors. When focusing on self-worth, therapists work with individuals to identify and challenge distorted beliefs about themselves, fostering a more positive self-concept. Through techniques like cognitive restructuring and behavior activation, individuals learn to combat negative self-perceptions and develop healthier coping strategies. Research indicates that improving self-worth through CBT interventions can lead to significant reductions in symptoms of depression, anxiety, and other mental health issues. By empowering individuals to challenge and reframe negative thoughts about themselves, CBT interventions targeting self-worth pave the way for lasting positive change in cognition, emotion, and behavior, ultimately enhancing overall psychological well-being.

The relationship between self-esteem and thought patterns

The relationship between self-esteem and thought patterns is a crucial aspect of CBT when addressing negative cognitions and behaviors. Individuals with low self-esteem often engage in maladaptive thinking patterns, such as self-criticism and catastrophizing, which can further fuel negative emotions and behaviors. CBT aims to challenge these distorted thought patterns by encouraging individuals to evaluate the evidence supporting their negative beliefs and replace them with more balanced and realistic interpretations of themselves and their experiences. Through techniques like cognitive restructuring and behavioral experiments, individuals can gradually shift their thought patterns to improve their self-esteem and overall well-being. By targeting the core beliefs underlying self-esteem issues, CBT helps individuals develop a more positive self-concept and cope effectively with challenges, ultimately leading to a more adaptive and fulfilling life.

Measuring changes in self-esteem post-CBT

Measuring changes in self-esteem post-CBT is a crucial aspect of evaluating the effectiveness of cognitive-behavioral therapy interventions. Self-esteem plays a pivotal role in individuals' overall psychological well-being and can significantly impact their ability to cope with negative thought patterns. By implementing structured assessment tools pre and post-CBT sessions, therapists can track changes in self-esteem levels and identify improvements in cognitive restructuring and emotional regulation. Tools such as the Rosenberg Self-Esteem Scale or the State Self-Esteem Scale provide quantitative measures to gauge shifts in self-perception and confidence levels. Analyzing these changes not only provides insights into the therapeutic process but also offers valuable data on the long-term efficacy of CBT in addressing negative thought patterns. Understanding the nuanced relationship between self-esteem and thought patterns post-CBT can further enhance therapeutic strategies and improve client outcomes in clinical practice.

XXI. PERSONALITY DISORDERS

CBT has been widely recognized for its efficacy in treating various mental health conditions, including personality disorders. The core focus of CBT on restructuring negative thought patterns aligns well with the distorted cognitions often present in individuals with personality disorders. Through the identification of maladaptive thoughts and beliefs, CBT aims to challenge and modify these cognitive distortions, thereby promoting more adaptive behaviors and improved emotional regulation. The application of CBT techniques, such as cognitive restructuring and behavioral experiments, can help individuals with personality disorders gain insight into their thought processes and develop healthier coping mechanisms. Despite challenges in treating personality disorders due to their ingrained nature, CBT has shown promising results in enhancing overall functioning and quality of life for individuals struggling with these complex conditions. Further research and tailored interventions in CBT for personality disorders may continue to advance the field and improve outcomes for this population.

Challenges in treating personality disorders

Personality disorders present a unique set of challenges in the context of CBT. Unlike more straightforward mental health conditions, personality disorders often involve deeply ingrained thought patterns and behaviors that are resistant to change. These individuals may struggle with issues such as emotional dysregulation, interpersonal difficulties, and a lack of insight into their own behaviors. Traditional CBT techniques, which focus on identifying and modifying specific negative thought patterns, may not always be sufficient in addressing the complexity of personality disorders. Therapists may need to adapt their approach, incorporating elements of dialectical behavior therapy or schema-focused therapy to effectively treat these individuals. The therapeutic relationship also plays a crucial role in navigating these challenges, as building trust and rapport with clients can be more challenging when working with personality disorders. Overall, treating personality disorders with CBT requires a nuanced and tailored approach to address the underlying cognitive and behavioral patterns that contribute to the disorder.

Adapting CBT for long-standing thought patterns

Adapting CBT for long-standing thought patterns requires a nuanced approach that integrates various techniques and methods to effectively address deeply ingrained negative schemas. While CBT typically focuses on identifying and challenging automatic negative thoughts, targeting more chronic and entrenched thought patterns necessitates a tailored and extended therapeutic process. Therapists may need to delve deeper into the origins and reinforcement mechanisms of these thoughts, utilizing techniques such as schema-focused therapy or narrative therapy to facilitate lasting change. Additionally, the integration of mindfulness practices and acceptance-based strategies can enhance the adaptability of CBT for individuals with persistent negative cognitive patterns. By expanding the traditional cognitive restructuring methods and incorporating a holistic approach, CBT can offer a comprehensive framework for long-term transformation of deeply rooted thought patterns, ultimately fostering significant improvements in mental well-being.

Outcomes of CBT in personality disorder treatment

The outcomes of CBT in the treatment of personality disorders have been extensively studied and documented. Research indicates that CBT is effective in facilitating significant improvements in individuals with personality disorders, particularly in terms of reducing maladaptive thought patterns and behaviors. Studies have shown that CBT helps individuals challenge distorted beliefs, develop healthier coping strategies, and enhance emotional regulation skills. By targeting negative thought patterns and dysfunctional behaviors, CBT enables individuals to modify their cognitive processing and responses to various situations. Ultimately, the goal of CBT in personality disorder treatment is to promote long-lasting change and improve overall functioning and quality of life for individuals. However, it is essential to note that the effectiveness of CBT may vary depending on the specific type and severity of the personality disorder, as well as individual factors such as motivation and willingness to engage in therapy. Further research and clinical trials are needed to continue enhancing the efficacy of CBT in treating personality disorders and further refining the therapeutic techniques used.

XXII. SUBSTANCE ABUSE

CBT and substance abuse present a complex relationship that requires specialized attention in clinical psychology. CBT, with its emphasis on changing negative thought patterns, plays a crucial role in addressing substance use disorders. By identifying and modifying maladaptive thoughts related to substance abuse, CBT can help individuals develop healthier coping mechanisms and behaviors. This therapeutic approach aims to challenge beliefs that contribute to addictive behaviors, ultimately promoting long-term recovery. Cognitive restructuring, problem-solving skills, and exposure techniques are commonly employed in CBT sessions to address substance abuse issues effectively. Empirical evidence supports the efficacy of CBT in treating substance-related disorders by targeting cognitive distortions and emotional dysregulation. Recognizing the significance of CBT in tackling substance abuse underscores the need for continued research and implementation of this therapeutic modality in addiction treatment programs.

Cognitive-behavioral models of addiction

Cognitive-behavioral models of addiction play a crucial role in understanding and treating substance use disorders. These models emphasize the interplay between cognitive processes, emotional responses, and behavioral patterns that contribute to addictive behaviors. By targeting maladaptive thoughts and beliefs associated with drug use, CBT aims to modify these negative cognitive patterns and ultimately change addictive behaviors. Through the identification of triggers, challenging irrational beliefs, and developing coping strategies, individuals can learn to manage cravings and avoid relapse. Research supports the effectiveness of CBT in addressing addiction, highlighting its role in promoting long-term recovery. By addressing the underlying cognitive processes driving substance abuse, CBT provides a comprehensive approach to addiction treatment that targets both the symptoms and root causes of the disorder, ultimately leading to sustainable behavior change.

CBT techniques for substance-related thoughts

In the realm of CBT, techniques aimed at addressing substance-related thoughts are crucial for the successful treatment of individuals struggling with addiction. Through cognitive restructuring, individuals can challenge and modify distorted beliefs and assumptions surrounding substance use. This process involves identifying triggers, examining the underlying thoughts and emotions associated with cravings, and developing healthier coping strategies to manage these triggers effectively. Additionally, techniques like problem-solving skills training equip individuals with the necessary tools to navigate challenging situations without resorting to substance use. Exposure therapy can also be utilized to help individuals confront and desensitize themselves to substance-related cues, ultimately reducing the power of these triggers over time. By implementing these CBT techniques in a tailored and comprehensive manner, clinicians can assist clients in reshaping their negative thought patterns and promoting long-lasting recovery from substance use disorders.

Effectiveness of CBT in addiction recovery

CBT has proven to be an effective method in addiction recovery by addressing negative thought patterns that contribute to substance abuse. By helping individuals recognize and reframe distorted thinking, CBT empowers them to develop healthier coping mechanisms and behaviors. Through cognitive restructuring and challenging irrational beliefs associated with addiction, CBT equips individuals with the tools needed to resist urges and make positive choices. Research shows that CBT significantly reduces relapse rates and improves long-term recovery outcomes. However, it is essential to consider the limitations of CBT, such as its reliance on individual commitment and the need for ongoing practice. Comparative studies with other therapy approaches like psychodynamic therapy highlight CBT's strengths in targeting specific cognitive processes underlying addiction. Overall, CBT's effectiveness in addiction recovery lies in its ability to address the root causes of substance abuse by reshaping destructive thought patterns towards lasting behavioral change.

XXIII. CHRONIC PAIN

Chronic pain is a pervasive issue with significant psychological repercussions, often fueling negative thought patterns and exacerbating the suffering of individuals. CBT has emerged as a promising approach to address the intertwined nature of chronic pain and cognitive distortions. By targeting maladaptive beliefs and restructuring cognitive processes, CBT aims to alleviate the impact of pain on an individual's mental well-being. Through strategies like cognitive restructuring and mindfulness techniques, CBT empowers individuals to challenge and replace negative thought patterns, fostering a more adaptive and resilient mindset in the face of chronic pain. Evidence suggests that CBT can significantly reduce pain-related distress, improve functional outcomes, and enhance overall quality of life for individuals grappling with chronic pain. This underscores the importance of integrating CBT into interdisciplinary treatment plans for chronic pain management, offering a holistic approach that addresses both the physical and psychological dimensions of pain.

Cognitive aspects of pain management

Cognitive aspects play a crucial role in the effective management of pain. CBT recognizes that how individuals interpret and think about their pain can either exacerbate or alleviate their suffering. By targeting negative thought patterns, CBT aims to restructure maladaptive beliefs and perceptions that contribute to the experience of pain. Through cognitive restructuring techniques, individuals learn to challenge and modify distorted cognitions regarding their pain, leading to a reduction in their distress levels and improved coping mechanisms. By addressing cognitive distortions and promoting adaptive thinking patterns, CBT empowers individuals to take control of their pain experience and increase their overall quality of life. Furthermore, by emphasizing the interconnectedness between thoughts, emotions, and behaviors, CBT provides a comprehensive approach to pain management that addresses the cognitive, emotional, and behavioral components of an individual's suffering.

CBT interventions for pain-related thoughts

One of the key components of CBT interventions for pain-related thoughts is cognitive restructuring. This method involves identifying and changing negative thought patterns that contribute to increased pain perception and distress. By challenging irrational beliefs and promoting more adaptive thinking, individuals can develop healthier cognitive patterns that ultimately reduce their experience of pain. Additionally, CBT techniques focus on educating individuals about the mind-body connection, helping them understand how thoughts and emotions can influence physical sensations. By incorporating relaxation techniques and stress management strategies, CBT interventions aim to enhance coping skills and improve overall well-being. Research suggests that CBT can effectively reduce pain intensity and disability in individuals with chronic pain conditions, highlighting its value in addressing both the psychological and physical aspects of pain management. As such, CBT interventions for pain-related thoughts offer a comprehensive and evidence-based approach to improving the quality of life for individuals experiencing chronic pain.

Research on CBT for chronic pain conditions

Research on CBT for chronic pain conditions has shown promising results in alleviating symptoms and improving overall quality of life for individuals suffering from persistent pain. A meta-analysis by Williams et al. (2012) found that CBT interventions led to significant reductions in pain intensity, disability, and distress in chronic pain patients. The effectiveness of CBT in managing chronic pain can be attributed to its focus on modifying maladaptive thought patterns and behaviors that contribute to pain perception and maintenance. By targeting cognitive distortions and promoting adaptive coping strategies, CBT helps individuals reframe their perceptions of pain and develop healthier ways of responding to it. The incorporation of mindfulness-based techniques and relaxation training further enhances the efficacy of CBT in chronic pain management. Future research should continue to explore the mechanisms through which CBT exerts its therapeutic effects on chronic pain conditions, ultimately contributing to the optimization of treatment protocols for individuals experiencing persistent pain.

XXIV. EATING DISORDERS

CBT has been increasingly recognized for its effectiveness in treating a range of psychological disorders, including eating disorders. In the context of addressing negative thought patterns associated with eating disorders, CBT offers a structured and goal-oriented approach that targets maladaptive beliefs, attitudes, and behaviors. By guiding individuals to identify and challenge distorted cognitions related to body image, food, and weight, CBT facilitates cognitive restructuring and the development of healthier coping strategies. Through techniques such as self-monitoring, behavioral experiments, and challenging cognitive distortions, individuals can gradually shift towards more adaptive thought patterns and behaviors. Empirical evidence supports the efficacy of CBT in reducing eating disorder symptoms and improving overall psychological well-being. However, further research is warranted to explore the long-term outcomes and adapt CBT techniques to address the complexities of eating disorders comprehensively.

The role of thoughts in eating behaviors

The role of thoughts in eating behaviors is a critical aspect of understanding and addressing disordered eating patterns. Within the framework of CBT, the impact of thoughts on eating behaviors is a central focus. Individuals with negative thought patterns relating to body image, food, and weight often engage in maladaptive eating behaviors as a result. Through CBT, these negative thought patterns are identified, challenged, and modified to promote healthier attitudes and behaviors surrounding food and body image. By recognizing the interconnected nature of thoughts, emotions, and behaviors, individuals undergoing CBT can learn to recognize and change their harmful thought patterns, leading to more positive and sustainable changes in their eating habits. The efficacy of CBT in treating eating disorders has been supported by empirical evidence, highlighting the significance of addressing thoughts in facilitating behavioral change and enhancing overall psychological well-being.

CBT strategies for disordered eating patterns

CBT offers effective strategies for addressing disordered eating patterns by targeting the negative thought processes that underlie these behaviors. Through cognitive restructuring, individuals are guided to identify and challenge their distorted beliefs about food, body image, and self-worth. By recognizing and changing these negative thoughts, individuals can alter their emotional responses and subsequently modify their eating behaviors. Additionally, CBT employs behavioral techniques such as exposure therapy and problem-solving skills to help individuals develop healthier coping mechanisms and responses to triggers. By integrating these cognitive and behavioral strategies, CBT aims to break the cycle of disordered eating patterns and promote lasting change. Research studies have shown the efficacy of CBT in addressing eating disorders such as bulimia nervosa and binge eating disorder, further supporting its role in transforming negative thought patterns associated with disordered eating. By targeting the underlying cognitive distortions and behaviors, CBT offers a comprehensive approach to promoting psychological well-being and lasting recovery from disordered eating patterns.

Treatment outcomes for eating disorders

Treatment outcomes for eating disorders within the realm of CBT have shown promising results. By addressing the maladaptive thoughts and behaviors that contribute to disordered eating, CBT aims to instill healthier coping mechanisms and improve overall well-being. Studies have indicated that CBT can lead to significant reductions in eating disorder symptomatology, with some individuals experiencing long-term remission. Through the identification and modification of negative thought patterns related to body image, self-worth, and food, individuals can develop a more positive relationship with themselves and their bodies. The structured nature of CBT, in conjunction with personalized treatment plans, allows for a targeted approach that addresses the specific challenges faced by each individual. Ultimately, the success of CBT in treating eating disorders underscores the importance of addressing cognitive factors in the therapeutic process.

XXV. SLEEP DISORDERS

CBT has proven to be a valuable tool in addressing sleep disorders, particularly by targeting negative thought patterns and maladaptive behaviors that contribute to sleep disturbances, CBT aims to improve sleep quality and overall well-being. This approach involves identifying and challenging dysfunctional beliefs about sleep, implementing relaxation techniques, establishing healthy sleep hygiene practices, and modifying behavior patterns that may disrupt sleep. Through cognitive restructuring and behavioral interventions, individuals can develop more adaptive coping strategies to manage stress and anxiety, leading to better sleep outcomes. Research studies have shown that CBT is effective in treating insomnia, with lasting improvements in sleep parameters. While limitations and criticisms exist, CBT's tailored approach to changing negative thought patterns makes it a promising option for individuals struggling with sleep disorders. Future research should further explore the nuances of CBT in addressing various types of sleep disturbances and its long-term impact on sleep quality.

Cognitive factors in insomnia

Cognitive factors play a significant role in the development and maintenance of factors such as dysfunctional beliefs about sleep, excessive worry, and rumination contribute to the perpetuation of sleep disturbances. Individuals with insomnia often exhibit cognitive biases, such as selective attention to sleep-related threats and catastrophic thinking about the consequences of poor sleep. These maladaptive beliefs and thought patterns can lead to hyperarousal, making it challenging for individuals to fall asleep or stay asleep. CBT targets these cognitive factors by helping individuals identify and challenge negative thought patterns related to sleep. Through cognitive restructuring techniques, individuals learn to reframe their thoughts, develop more adaptive beliefs about sleep, and reduce excessive rumination. By addressing these cognitive factors, CBT can effectively improve sleep quality and treat insomnia in the long term.

CBT for sleep-related thought patterns

CBT has been widely utilized in clinical psychology for its effectiveness in modifying negative thought patterns, including those related to sleep. By addressing the interconnection between thoughts, emotions, and behaviors, CBT offers a structured approach to identify and challenge maladaptive beliefs. In the context of sleep-related thought patterns, CBT aims to interrupt the cycle of rumination and anxiety that often contribute to techniques such as cognitive restructuring, where individuals learn to reframe negative thoughts about sleep, and sleep hygiene practices help individuals develop more adaptive attitudes towards sleep. Research has shown that CBT for sleep disorders leads to significant improvements in sleep quality and duration. By targeting negative thought patterns, CBT not only alleviates sleep disturbances but also promotes overall psychological well-being. Future research could further explore the mechanisms underlying these cognitive interventions and their long-term efficacy in maintaining healthy sleep patterns.

Effectiveness of CBT for insomnia

While CBT has been widely recognized for its effectiveness in treating various mental health conditions, its efficacy in addressing insomnia warrants further exploration. CBT for insomnia, or CBT-I, focuses on changing negative thought patterns and behaviors that contribute to sleep disturbances. By targeting dysfunctional beliefs about sleep and implementing techniques such as cognitive restructuring and sleep hygiene education, CBT-I aims to improve sleep quality and quantity without the use of medication. Research studies have shown promising results, with CBT-I demonstrating comparable or superior outcomes to pharmacological interventions in the long-term management, however, some limitations exist, including accessibility issues and the need for trained practitioners. Despite these challenges, the evidence supporting the effectiveness of CBT for insomnia underscores its value in promoting healthy sleep habits and improving overall well-being. Future research should continue to explore innovative methods to enhance the delivery and accessibility of CBT-I to maximize its benefits for individuals struggling with insomnia.

XXVI. ANGER MANAGEMENT

CBT has proven to be an effective approach in addressing issues related to anger management. By targeting negative thought patterns and maladaptive behaviors, CBT aims to restructure cognitive processes that contribute to anger outbursts. This form of therapy helps individuals identify triggering thoughts, challenging distorted beliefs, and developing healthier coping strategies. Through techniques such as cognitive restructuring and problem-solving, CBT enables individuals to manage their emotions more effectively and respond to anger-provoking situations in a more adaptive manner. Research has shown that CBT can significantly reduce anger levels and aggression, leading to improved overall well-being. By understanding the interplay between thoughts, emotions, and behaviors, individuals undergoing CBT for anger management can experience long-lasting positive changes in their emotional regulation and interpersonal relationships. These findings highlight the vital role CBT plays in addressing anger issues and promoting healthier coping mechanisms.

Understanding anger through CBT

Understanding anger through CBT involves unraveling the intricate web of thoughts, emotions, and behaviors that contribute to this intense emotional response. CBT, with its empirical foundation and practical techniques, offers a structured approach to identify and modify key cognitive distortions associated with anger. By examining the core beliefs and automatic thoughts fueling the individual's anger, CBT allows for the development of healthier coping strategies and more adaptive behaviors. Through cognitive restructuring and challenging maladaptive beliefs, individuals can reframe their perception of anger-provoking situations, leading to more constructive responses. CBT's emphasis on problem-solving and exposure techniques further aids in reshaping one's behavioral responses to anger triggers. Overall, CBT provides a comprehensive framework for understanding and addressing anger, highlighting the interconnected nature of thoughts, emotions, and actions in the manifestation of this powerful emotion.

Techniques for modifying anger-related thoughts

In CBT, techniques for modifying anger-related thoughts play a pivotal role in promoting emotional regulation and overall well-being. One of the primary techniques employed in CBT is cognitive restructuring, which involves identifying and challenging irrational or negative thought patterns associated with anger. By encouraging individuals to question and reframe their beliefs, CBT helps them develop more balanced and constructive perspectives on anger-provoking situations. Additionally, problem-solving strategies are utilized to address underlying issues contributing to anger, enhancing coping skills and reducing the intensity of emotional reactions. Moreover, exposure techniques are employed to desensitize individuals to triggers of anger and develop effective behavioral responses. Through these evidence-based techniques, CBT equips individuals with the tools to manage anger-related thoughts successfully, leading to improved emotional regulation and enhanced psychological wellbeing.

Efficacy of CBT in managing anger

CBT has been widely recognized for its efficacy in managing anger by targeting negative thought patterns. By helping individuals identify and challenge their irrational beliefs and distorted thinking, CBT aims to reframe their perspectives and change maladaptive behaviors. Through the implementation of cognitive restructuring techniques, individuals learn to replace negative self-talk with more constructive interpretations, leading to a reduction in anger-related triggers and impulsive reactions. Additionally, the incorporation of behavioral interventions, such as relaxation exercises and anger management skills, provides practical tools to cope with challenging situations. Research studies have consistently shown the effectiveness of CBT in addressing anger issues by promoting healthier thought processes and enhancing emotional regulation. However, criticisms of CBT suggest that its focus on cognitive restructuring may overlook underlying emotional issues. Despite these limitations, CBT remains a valuable therapeutic approach in managing anger and fostering long-term emotional well-being.

XXVII. THE WORKPLACE

In the workplace, the implementation of CBT has been gaining momentum as a powerful tool for modifying negative thought patterns and improving overall well-being among employees. By understanding the interplay between thoughts, emotions, and behaviors, CBT equips individuals with practical techniques to challenge and reframe maladaptive thoughts. Through cognitive restructuring and problem-solving strategies, employees can learn to identify and replace negative thought patterns with more constructive and positive beliefs. Furthermore, the exposure techniques utilized in CBT help individuals confront their fears and anxieties in a controlled environment, facilitating gradual desensitization. Research studies have shown the efficacy of CBT in treating work-related stress, anxiety, and depression, highlighting its potential to enhance productivity and job satisfaction. As organizations prioritize employee mental health, integrating CBT interventions in the workplace can foster a more positive and resilient workforce, ultimately contributing to a healthier organizational culture and increased overall psychological well-being.

Addressing work-related stress and thoughts

Work-related stress can often lead to negative thought patterns that can significantly impact an individual's well-being and productivity. In the context of CBT, addressing these negative thoughts is a fundamental aspect of treatment. By examining the interplay between thoughts, emotions, and behaviors, CBT aims to identify and challenge maladaptive thought patterns that contribute to stress and anxiety in the workplace. Through techniques like cognitive restructuring and problem-solving, individuals can learn to reframe their thinking, leading to more positive emotions and adaptive behaviors in response to work-related stressors. By effectively changing these negative thought patterns, CBT equips individuals with the skills needed to manage stress more effectively, ultimately improving their overall psychological well-being and work performance. Future research in this area could further explore the efficacy of CBT in addressing specific work-related stressors and optimizing professional functioning.

CBT programs for employee well-being

CBT programs have increasingly gained attention for promoting employee well-being by addressing negative thought patterns. By utilizing cognitive restructuring, problem-solving techniques, and exposure therapy, CBT aims to modify maladaptive cognitions and behaviors that contribute to stress and burnout in the workplace. These interventions focus on identifying cognitive distortions, challenging them with evidence-based reasoning, and implementing healthier coping strategies. Research supports the efficacy of CBT in reducing symptoms of anxiety and depression among employees, ultimately enhancing their psychological resilience and overall job performance. However, it is essential to acknowledge the limitations of CBT, such as its time-intensive nature and the need for ongoing practice to maintain therapeutic gains. Incorporating CBT programs into organizational wellness initiatives can offer long-term benefits by equipping employees with valuable skills to navigate workplace challenges and foster a positive mental health culture. Further research is warranted to explore the long-term effects of CBT on employee well-being and productivity.

Studies on the impact of CBT in occupational settings

Studies on the impact of CBT in occupational settings have shown promising results in enhancing psychological well-being and performance amongst employees. Research has indicated that CBT interventions in workplace environments can effectively address negative thought patterns that may lead to high levels of stress, anxiety, and burnout. By targeting maladaptive thinking styles and behavior patterns, CBT equips individuals with practical strategies to challenge and reframe negative beliefs, fostering a more positive and resilient mindset. Moreover, the application of CBT techniques, such as cognitive restructuring and problem-solving, has demonstrated significant improvements in coping mechanisms and stress management skills among employees. These findings suggest that integrating CBT into occupational settings can not only enhance individual psychological health but also contribute to a more productive and supportive work environment overall. Further research in this area could explore the long-term effects of CBT interventions within specific industries and evaluate their potential for sustainable mental health promotion in the workplace.

XXVIII. TRAINING AND SUPERVISION

In addressing XXVIII. Training and Supervision in CBT, it is essential to consider the pivotal role that proper training and supervision play in enhancing therapeutic outcomes. Training programs for CBT therapists typically encompass theoretical knowledge, practical skills, and supervised clinical experience. Adequate training ensures therapists have a sound understanding of the cognitive model, techniques for identifying and modifying negative thought patterns, and the ability to establish a strong therapeutic alliance with clients. Moreover, ongoing supervision allows therapists to receive feedback on their clinical work, enhance their competence, and maintain fidelity to the CBT model. The supervision process facilitates the discussion of challenging cases, fosters professional growth, and ensures that therapists adhere to ethical guidelines. Ultimately, rigorous training and supervision in CBT are crucial for promoting successful therapeutic interventions and improving client outcomes.

Requirements for CBT practitioners

In fulfilling the requirements for CBT practitioners, a multi-faceted skill set is essential. Firstly, practitioners must have a solid understanding of CBT principles, including the intricate relationship between thoughts, emotions, and behaviors. This foundational knowledge will enable them to effectively identify and challenge negative thought patterns in clients. Additionally, CBT practitioners must possess exceptional communication and interpersonal skills to establish trust and rapport with clients, creating a conducive therapeutic environment. Moreover, proficiency in various CBT techniques such as cognitive restructuring, problem-solving, and exposure therapy is imperative for practitioners to successfully guide clients in changing their negative thought patterns. Lastly, ongoing training and education in the latest developments in CBT research and practices are necessary to ensure practitioners deliver evidence-based and effective interventions. Ultimately, a comprehensive skill set combined with a commitment to professional growth is essential for CBT practitioners to effectively facilitate change in their clients' negative thought patterns.

Models of CBT supervision

Models of CBT supervision play a crucial role in ensuring the effectiveness and quality of therapy provided by clinicians. One prevalent model is the developmental supervision model, focusing on the growth and skill acquisition of the therapist throughout their career. This model emphasizes the importance of ongoing feedback, guidance, and support to enhance the therapist's competence in delivering CBT. Another commonly used model is the cognitive-behavioral approach to supervision, which mirrors the principles of CBT itself, emphasizing collaboration, active problem-solving, and skills training. This model aims to address specific challenges faced by therapists, such as managing difficult cases or dealing with countertransference issues. By implementing these models effectively, supervisors can not only support therapists in developing their skills but also ensure that clients receive high-quality and evidence-based therapy to effectively change their negative thought patterns.

Ensuring fidelity to the CBT model

Ensuring fidelity to the CBT model is paramount in achieving successful outcomes when tackling negative thought patterns. Therapists must adhere closely to the core principles and techniques of CBT to effectively challenge maladaptive beliefs and behaviors. One critical aspect of maintaining fidelity involves continuous training and supervision for therapists to ensure they apply the interventions correctly and consistently. Moreover, therapists must tailor interventions to the individual needs of each client, considering their unique cognitive distortions and emotional triggers. Regular assessment and feedback mechanisms can help in monitoring progress and making necessary adjustments to the treatment plan. By staying true to the foundations of CBT and adapting strategies based on client feedback, therapists can maximize the effectiveness of interventions in reshaping negative thought patterns. This fidelity ultimately enhances the therapeutic alliance and promotes lasting behavioral change in clients.

XXIX. ETHICAL CONSIDERATIONS

Ethical considerations are paramount in the practice of CBT due to the unique nature of the therapeutic relationship and the interventions employed. While CBT is evidence-based and goal-oriented, therapists must navigate ethical dilemmas to ensure the well-being and autonomy of their clients. Issues such as confidentiality, informed consent, and boundaries become particularly salient when working to change negative thought patterns in clients. Therapists must maintain professional boundaries, ensure clients understand the risks and benefits of treatment, and respect their autonomy throughout the therapeutic process. Additionally, cultural sensitivity and awareness of power differentials are crucial in CBT to promote the ethical delivery of therapy. By upholding ethical standards, CBT practitioners can effectively facilitate positive change in clients while safeguarding their rights and well-being.

Informed consent and confidentiality

Informed consent and confidentiality are two fundamental ethical principles that are crucial in the practice of CBT. The beginning of any therapeutic relationship must involve obtaining the client's informed consent, ensuring that they fully understand the nature of the therapy, its potential benefits, and any risks involved. This process sets the foundation for trust and collaboration between the therapist and client. Moving into the middle of the paragraph, confidentiality plays a key role in maintaining this trust, as clients must feel assured that their personal information will be kept private and secure. Breaches of confidentiality can have detrimental effects on the therapeutic alliance and may impede the client's progress. To ensure ethical conduct, therapists must adhere to strict guidelines regarding confidentiality, only breaking it in cases of imminent harm to the client or others. In conclusion, a strong emphasis on informed consent and confidentiality is essential in CBT to foster a safe and trusting therapeutic environment where clients can feel comfortable exploring and changing their negative thought patterns.

Managing dual relationships and boundaries

In the realm of CBT, managing dual relationships and boundaries is a crucial aspect that demands careful consideration. Therapists must navigate the intricate balance between establishing a therapeutic alliance with their clients while maintaining professional boundaries to avoid conflicts of interest or ethical dilemmas. Dual relationships, where the therapist and client may have contact outside of therapy, can potentially blur the lines between personal and professional relationships, undermining the therapeutic process. By setting clear boundaries from the onset and consistently reinforcing them, therapists can uphold the integrity of the therapeutic relationship and minimize the risk of harm to the client. Furthermore, understanding the dynamics of dual relationships and actively managing potential conflicts can foster a safe and effective therapeutic environment conducive to meaningful change in negative thought patterns. It is through this delicate dance of connection and detachment that CBT practitioners can effectively support their clients on the path to cognitive restructuring and emotional healing.

Ethical dilemmas specific to CBT

Ethical dilemmas specific to CBT can arise due to the nature of challenging and modifying deeply ingrained negative thought patterns in patients. One key dilemma involves the issue of informed consent, as therapists must ensure that clients understand the purpose and potential risks of CBT before proceeding with treatment. Additionally, maintaining boundaries and avoiding dual relationships can be challenging in CBT, especially when delving into personal and sensitive topics. Therapists must navigate the ethical implications of influencing and potentially altering a client's core beliefs and self-perception. Furthermore, the use of cognitive restructuring techniques may inadvertently challenge a client's cultural beliefs or values, raising concerns about cultural competence and sensitivity. Ultimately, therapists must continuously reflect on their ethical responsibilities to prioritize the well-being and autonomy of their clients while effectively implementing CBT techniques to promote positive changes in thought patterns.

XXX. MEASURING OUTCOMES

Measuring outcomes in CBT plays a vital role in assessing the effectiveness of this therapeutic approach in changing negative thought patterns. Various outcome measures are used to evaluate the progress of clients undergoing CBT, including self-report questionnaires, behavioral observations, and clinician ratings. These measurements provide valuable insights into the reduction of negative thinking, improvement in mood, and changes in behaviors that align with treatment goals. By utilizing standardized assessment tools and conducting thorough evaluations, therapists can track the client's progress over time and tailor interventions accordingly. Moreover, outcome measures in CBT not only help in gauging the effectiveness of the therapy but also contribute to enhancing treatment outcomes and optimizing therapeutic interventions. Overall, the utilization of outcome measures in CBT serves as a pivotal component in fostering positive changes in individuals grappling with negative thought patterns, leading to better psychological well-being and improved quality of life.

Tools for assessing thought change

A vital aspect of CBT is the use of tools for assessing thought change. One key tool is cognitive restructuring, which involves challenging and changing negative thought patterns through the examination of evidence for and against these patterns. By identifying cognitive distortions and replacing them with more balanced and realistic thoughts, individuals can alter their perceptions and reactions to stressors. Another effective method is problem-solving, where individuals learn to approach challenges in a systematic and goal-oriented manner, thereby reducing feelings of helplessness and hopelessness. Additionally, exposure techniques help individuals confront their fears gradually, enabling them to reevaluate and update their beliefs about the perceived threat. These tools, when applied in a structured and collaborative therapeutic setting, empower individuals to develop adaptive thought patterns and ultimately improve their mental well-being. Through conscious effort and practice, individuals can successfully modify their negative thought patterns with the guidance of CBT techniques.

The importance of measuring treatment efficacy

Measuring treatment efficacy in CBT is of paramount importance in the field of clinical psychology. By systematically assessing the effectiveness of interventions, therapists can ensure that their patients are benefiting from the treatment and make informed decisions about their care. Through measures like symptom reduction, behavioral changes, and improved quality of life, practitioners can track progress and adjust treatment plans accordingly. Additionally, outcome measures in CBT allow researchers to evaluate the overall impact of the therapy and contribute to the growing body of empirical evidence supporting its efficacy. The ability to quantify the outcomes of CBT not only helps clinicians tailor interventions to individual needs but also strengthens the credibility of the approach in a field that values evidence-based practices. Ultimately, measuring treatment efficacy in CBT not only enhances the effectiveness of the therapy but also underscores its significance in promoting positive psychological well-being.

Challenges in outcome research

Challenges in outcome research in the realm of CBT present a complex landscape for practitioners and researchers. The dynamic nature of human cognition and behavior adds a layer of intricacy when measuring the efficacy of interventions designed to alter negative thought patterns. One key challenge lies in the subjective nature of outcomes, as individuals may interpret and report their progress differently based on various factors. Additionally, the diversity of presenting issues and individual differences further complicate the standardization of assessment tools and outcome measures in CBT research. This variability poses a threat to the reliability and generalizability of findings within the field. Moreover, the long-term sustainability of positive changes in thought patterns over time presents a hurdle that requires longitudinal studies and follow-up assessments to accurately capture the impact and durability of CBT interventions. Addressing these challenges through rigorous study design, standardized assessment protocols, and longitudinal follow-ups is crucial in advancing the empirical evidence base for CBT and enhancing its effectiveness in changing negative thought patterns.

XXXI. LIMITATIONS AND CRITICISMS

While CBT has garnered widespread acclaim for its efficacy in changing negative thought patterns, it is not without its limitations and criticisms. One prominent critique of CBT is that it may oversimplify complex psychological issues by focusing solely on surface-level symptoms rather than underlying causes. Critics argue that this approach may be insufficient for individuals with deep-seated traumas or unresolved emotional conflicts. Additionally, some research suggests that CBT's effects may not always be long-lasting, with individuals experiencing relapses after completing therapy. Another criticism is that CBT may not be suitable for all individuals, particularly those with severe mental health conditions or cognitive impairments. Despite these limitations, it is essential to acknowledge that CBT remains a valuable therapeutic tool, but must be further refined and supplemented with additional modalities to address its shortcomings effectively.

Potential shortcomings of CBT

Despite its proven efficacy in treating various psychological disorders, CBT is not without potential shortcomings. One significant criticism of CBT is its focus on symptom reduction rather than exploring deeper underlying causes of negative thought patterns. This limitation may result in the temporary alleviation of symptoms without addressing the root causes, leading to potential relapses in the future. Additionally, some individuals may find CBT overly structured and directive, potentially hindering the development of a strong therapeutic alliance between the client and the therapist. This lack of a strong therapeutic relationship could affect the overall effectiveness of the intervention. Moreover, the emphasis on cognitive restructuring in CBT may not be suitable for everyone, as some individuals may benefit more from interventions that focus on emotional processing or interpersonal dynamics. Despite these shortcomings, CBT remains a valuable and widely used therapeutic approach in clinical psychology, with ongoing research aimed at addressing these limitations to enhance its effectiveness in changing negative thought patterns.

Critiques from other therapeutic approaches

Critiques from other therapeutic approaches can provide valuable insights into the effectiveness and limitations of CBT in changing negative thought patterns. While CBT has been widely praised for its evidence-based approach and structured techniques, it has faced criticisms from alternative therapeutic modalities. For instance, psychodynamic therapy emphasizes the exploration of unconscious motivations and childhood experiences, arguing that cognitive restructuring alone may not address deeper-rooted issues. ACT suggests that changing the relationship with negative thoughts, rather than solely modifying them, is key to long-lasting change. These critiques suggest that while CBT is effective in addressing cognitive distortions, it may not always delve deep enough into the underlying causes of negative thinking patterns. Acknowledging these critiques can help therapists adapt and refine CBT interventions to better meet the diverse needs of clients seeking to change their negative thought patterns.

Addressing the limitations in practice

Addressing the limitations in practice is a crucial aspect when implementing CBT in clinical settings. While CBT has been proven effective in changing negative thought patterns and improving psychological well-being, it is essential to acknowledge its limitations. One major limitation is the issue of treatment resistance, where some individuals may not respond well to CBT interventions. In such cases, therapists need to explore alternative therapeutic approaches or tailor the CBT techniques to better suit the individual's needs. Additionally, the lack of accessibility to qualified CBT practitioners in certain regions can hinder the widespread adoption of CBT as a primary treatment option. Efforts to train more therapists in CBT and increase awareness of its benefits are necessary to overcome this limitation. By addressing these challenges, practitioners can better optimize the effectiveness of CBT in changing negative thought patterns and promoting mental health.

XXXII. FUTURE DIRECTIONS IN CBT RESEARCH

Moving forward, the field of CBT is poised for numerous exciting avenues of exploration. One particular area of interest lies in the personalized application of CBT techniques, tailoring interventions to individual needs and characteristics. This approach could enhance treatment outcomes by addressing unique thought patterns and behaviors more effectively. Moreover, integrating technology into CBT delivery, such as mobile applications or virtual reality platforms, holds promise in increasing accessibility and effectiveness. Another direction for research involves investigating the neural mechanisms underlying CBT's impact on changing negative thought patterns, shedding light on the neurobiological underpinnings of cognitive restructuring. Furthermore, examining the long-term effects of CBT beyond symptom reduction to focus on fostering resilience and well-being would be a valuable pursuit. These future directions in CBT research have the potential to deepen our understanding of its mechanisms and enhance its therapeutic benefits for a wide range of psychological conditions.

Emerging trends and innovations

In the realm of CBT and the endeavor to alter negative thought patterns, emerging trends and innovations are continually shaping the landscape of therapeutic interventions. As advancements in technology provide new avenues for mental health treatment, virtual reality programs are being integrated into CBT practices to simulate real-world scenarios and aid in exposure therapy. Additionally, machine learning algorithms are being utilized to personalize treatment plans by analyzing vast amounts of data and identifying patterns that may be missed by human clinicians. These innovations not only enhance the efficacy of CBT in targeting negative thought patterns but also contribute to the evolution of the therapeutic process by offering tailored and immersive experiences for clients. By embracing these emerging trends, practitioners can further refine their techniques and optimize outcomes in the challenging endeavor of changing deeply ingrained negative thought patterns.

The need for long-term follow-up studies

One critical aspect concerning CBT that warrants attention is the necessity for long-term follow-up studies to assess the lasting impacts of intervention. While the efficacy of CBT in changing negative thought patterns has been well-established through numerous short-term studies, the sustainability of these changes over time remains less clear. Longitudinal studies are crucial in determining whether the cognitive restructuring and behavioral modifications achieved during therapy persist beyond the treatment period. Understanding the long-term effects of CBT is paramount in evaluating its overall effectiveness in promoting enduring positive mental health outcomes. By tracking individuals post-treatment, researchers can assess the durability of the cognitive shifts and behavioral adaptations instilled during therapy, thereby providing valuable insights into the maintenance of these changes in real-life settings. In essence, long-term follow-up studies are essential in validating the efficacy of CBT in fostering lasting transformations in individuals' thought patterns and behaviors.

Expanding the evidence base for CBT

Expanding the evidence base for CBT is crucial in advancing its effectiveness in changing negative thought patterns. Research studies have shown that CBT can be tailored to diverse populations and various mental health conditions, highlighting its versatility and applicability. By continuously exploring new methods and techniques within CBT, such as incorporating technology-based interventions or culturally sensitive approaches, therapists can enhance treatment outcomes and reach a broader range of individuals. Additionally, ongoing empirical research helps identify the most effective strategies for targeting specific negative thought patterns, offering valuable insights into the mechanisms underlying cognitive restructuring and behavioral activation. By expanding the evidence base for CBT, clinicians can refine their practice and contribute to the evolution of this therapeutic approach, ultimately improving mental health outcomes for individuals facing cognitive distortions and negative thinking patterns.

XXXIII. RESILIENCE BUILDING

In the pursuit of resilience building, CBT has emerged as a powerful tool. By targeting negative thought patterns, CBT equips individuals with the skills to identify and challenge maladaptive beliefs, ultimately fostering more adaptive coping strategies. Through the process of cognitive restructuring, individuals can learn to reframe their perceptions of themselves, others, and the world around them, leading to a more balanced and realistic outlook. Problem-solving techniques employed in CBT help individuals navigate challenging situations more effectively, empowering them to take proactive steps towards resolution. Furthermore, exposure therapy within CBT allows individuals to confront feared situations gradually, thereby reducing anxiety and building resilience. By integrating these methods and techniques, CBT plays a crucial role in enhancing individuals' ability to bounce back from adversity and lead more fulfilling lives.

Strengthening coping strategies through CBT

One of the key strengths of CBT lies in its ability to equip individuals with effective coping strategies to manage and change negative thought patterns. By utilizing cognitive restructuring techniques, individuals can challenge and replace maladaptive thoughts with more rational and constructive alternatives. This process involves identifying automatic negative thoughts, evaluating their validity and impact, and ultimately restructuring them to promote healthier beliefs and behaviors. Through the implementation of problem-solving skills and exposure therapy, CBT empowers individuals to confront their fears and anxieties, gradually desensitizing them and fostering resilience. Research studies have consistently shown the efficacy of CBT in treating various mental health conditions by targeting and modifying negative thought patterns. By strengthening coping strategies through CBT, individuals can cultivate a more adaptive mindset, enhancing their psychological well-being and overall quality of life.

CBT's role in fostering psychological resilience

CBT plays a crucial role in fostering psychological resilience by targeting and changing negative thought patterns. Through the interrelation of thoughts, emotions, and behaviors, CBT aims to restructure maladaptive thoughts and beliefs that contribute to distress and dysfunction. By challenging automatic negative thoughts and implementing cognitive restructuring techniques, individuals can develop healthier perspectives and coping strategies. The empirical evidence supporting CBT's effectiveness in treating various mental health disorders, such as depression and anxiety, underscores its efficacy in promoting resilience and improving overall well-being. Furthermore, CBT's emphasis on practical skills, problem-solving, and goal-setting equips individuals with the tools necessary to navigate adversity and challenges with greater resilience. Ultimately, CBT empowers individuals to cultivate adaptive thought patterns and behaviors, enhancing their psychological flexibility and capacity to withstand life's stressors.

Studies on resilience outcomes post-CBT

Studies on resilience outcomes post-CBT highlight the substantial impact of cognitive behavioral therapy in fostering individuals' capacity to cope with adversity. Research has shown that individuals who undergo CBT exhibit enhanced resilience in the face of stressors, demonstrating a reduced susceptibility to negative thought patterns and heightened emotional regulation skills. For instance, a study by Meichenbaum and Cameron (2017) illustrated that individuals with anxiety disorders who received CBT exhibited greater levels of resilience and reduced cognitive distortions compared to those who did not undergo treatment. This suggests that CBT not only targets and modifies negative thought patterns but also instills lasting changes that contribute to improved psychological well-being. These findings underscore the enduring benefits of CBT in promoting resilience and highlight its effectiveness in fostering adaptive coping strategies post-treatment.

XXXIV. RELAPSE PREVENTION

CBT is a powerful therapeutic tool in clinical psychology, with a primary aim of changing negative thought patterns that contribute to psychological distress. One crucial aspect in maintaining progress and preventing relapse after undergoing CBT is the integration of relapse prevention strategies. CBT and Relapse Prevention involves identifying triggers and warning signs that may lead to a return of negative thought patterns and equips individuals with coping mechanisms to effectively manage these challenges. By focusing on building resilience and developing adaptive thinking patterns through continued practice of cognitive restructuring and problem-solving techniques, individuals are better prepared to navigate potential setbacks. Integrating relapse prevention strategies into CBT not only reinforces positive changes but also empowers individuals to recognize and address potential obstacles on their path towards lasting psychological well-being. These strategies serve as a valuable component in sustaining the benefits of CBT over the long term.

Strategies for maintaining cognitive gains

Strategies for maintaining cognitive gains in CBT are vital to the long-term success of treatment. One essential strategy is regular practice and repetition of the learned techniques. Consistent engagement with cognitive restructuring exercises, problem-solving methods, and exposure therapies can strengthen neural pathways associated with positive thought patterns. Additionally, setting realistic goals and tracking progress can provide motivation and reinforcement for cognitive gains. Integrating mindfulness practices into daily routines can further enhance awareness of thought patterns and promote emotional regulation. Lastly, developing a strong support system and seeking follow-up sessions with a therapist can provide ongoing guidance and accountability. By implementing these strategies, individuals undergoing CBT can sustain their cognitive gains over time, leading to lasting improvements in mental health and overall well-being.

Preventing the return of negative thought patterns

Preventing the return of negative thought patterns is crucial in maintaining the progress made through CBT. One effective strategy is to teach clients to recognize and challenge their Automatic Negative Thoughts (ANTs) continually. By cultivating mindfulness and awareness of these patterns, individuals can intercept and reframe these thoughts before they spiral into negative emotions and behaviors. Additionally, implementing cognitive restructuring techniques, such as thought records and cognitive reframing, can help alter deeply ingrained negative beliefs. It is essential for therapists to equip their clients with coping strategies to cope with setbacks and prevent relapses. By building resilience and self-awareness, individuals can navigate challenging situations without succumbing to old thought patterns. Ultimately, vigilance, practice, and a commitment to ongoing reflection are essential in preventing negative thought patterns from resurfacing and maintaining mental well-being.

Research on the durability of CBT effects

Research on the durability of CBT effects is crucial in understanding the long-term benefits of this therapeutic approach in changing negative thought patterns. Studies have shown that CBT not only aids in immediate symptom relief but also equips individuals with long-lasting coping strategies. Research by Hofmann et al. (2012) emphasizes the maintenance of treatment gains post-therapy, suggesting that the skills learned during CBT sessions can be retained and applied beyond the therapy setting. Additionally, a meta-analysis by Butler et al. (2006) found that the effects of CBT endure over time, indicating its effectiveness in preventing relapse. However, some researchers have raised concerns regarding the lack of follow-up studies in this area, urging further investigation into the lasting impact of CBT on individuals' mental health. Therefore, continuous research on the durability of CBT effects is essential in validating its efficacy and informing future clinical practice.

XXXV. COMBINATION WITH MEDICATION

When discussing the application of CBT in conjunction with medication, it is essential to evaluate the synergistic effects of these two treatment modalities. While CBT primarily focuses on changing negative thought patterns by addressing cognitions and behaviors, medication targets the biological aspects of mental health conditions. Combining these approaches can lead to enhanced outcomes for individuals struggling with disorders like depression and anxiety. Research has shown that the combination of CBT and medication can be more effective than either intervention alone, particularly for those with severe symptoms. By integrating psychosocial and pharmacological treatments, individuals may experience faster relief and long-term benefits. However, it is crucial to consider individual differences, potential side effects, and the need for ongoing monitoring and adjustment in such combined treatments. Future studies should continue to explore the optimal strategies for integrating CBT and medication to maximize therapeutic outcomes and improve overall psychological well-being.

The debate over combined treatment approaches

The debate over combined treatment approaches in the realm of CBT is a topic that has garnered significant attention in recent years. While CBT has been widely recognized for its efficacy in changing negative thought patterns, there are ongoing discussions regarding the benefits of combining CBT with other therapeutic modalities. Proponents argue that integrated treatments, such as CBT combined with mindfulness-based interventions or pharmacotherapy, can enhance outcomes and provide more comprehensive support to individuals with complex mental health needs. On the other hand, critics express concerns about the potential dilution of CBT principles and the risk of information overload for clients. By carefully weighing the advantages and drawbacks of combined treatment approaches, clinicians can tailor interventions to best meet the unique needs of each individual, ultimately maximizing the effectiveness of therapy in addressing negative thought patterns.

Research on the efficacy of CBT and pharmacotherapy

Research on the efficacy of CBT and pharmacotherapy has shown promising results in the treatment of various mental health disorders. Studies have indicated that CBT is highly effective in modifying negative thought patterns by targeting the underlying cognitive distortions that contribute to emotional distress and maladaptive behaviors. By challenging and restructuring these negative thoughts, individuals can experience significant improvements in their symptoms and overall well-being. Furthermore, CBT has been found to have lasting benefits, reducing the likelihood of relapse compared to pharmacotherapy alone. While pharmacotherapy can be an important tool in managing symptoms, CBT offers a more holistic approach by addressing the root causes of negative thought patterns. Overall, the combination of CBT and pharmacotherapy can provide a comprehensive treatment approach for individuals struggling with mental health issues.

Clinical guidelines for combined treatments

Clinical guidelines for combined treatments in addressing negative thought patterns involve the integration of CBT with other therapeutic modalities to enhance treatment outcomes. In the initial phases of therapy, it is crucial to conduct a comprehensive assessment of the individual's cognitive distortions and negative beliefs. Once these patterns are identified, a combination of CBT techniques, such as cognitive restructuring and behavioral activation, can be integrated with other evidence-based interventions like mindfulness-based therapy or pharmacotherapy. By combining these approaches, clinicians can target multiple aspects of the individual's psychological distress simultaneously, facilitating a more holistic and effective treatment approach. However, it is essential for practitioners to carefully tailor the combined treatment plan to suit the specific needs and strengths of each client while remaining mindful of the potential challenges and limitations associated with integrating different therapeutic approaches.

XXXVI. LIFE TRANSITIONS

Life transitions, whether expected or unexpected, can be challenging and often lead to the onset or exacerbation of negative thought patterns. CBT offers a structured and evidence-based approach to navigating these transitions by modifying maladaptive cognitions. By challenging distorted beliefs and encouraging adaptive thinking, CBT equips individuals with the tools to cope effectively with life changes. Through the examination of thought-behavior-emotion cycles, CBT helps individuals identify and replace negative schemas with more positive and realistic alternatives, fostering resilience and psychological well-being. Techniques such as cognitive restructuring and problem-solving empower individuals to reframe situations and approach transitions with a more constructive mindset. In conclusion, CBT's focus on altering negative thought patterns during life transitions underscores its efficacy in promoting adaptive coping strategies and psychosocial adjustment. Further research in this area can enhance our understanding of how CBT can optimize psychological outcomes during times of change.

Navigating changes using CBT principles

Navigating changes using CBT principles entails a systematic approach to modifying negative thought patterns that contribute to emotional distress and maladaptive behaviors. By incorporating the basic principles of CBT, individuals can learn to recognize the interplay between their thoughts, emotions, and actions, thus gaining insight into the cognitive distortions fueling their negative beliefs. Techniques such as cognitive restructuring, problem-solving, and exposure are employed in therapy sessions to challenge and reframe these distorted thoughts, paving the way for more adaptive patterns of thinking. Through empirical evidence supporting the efficacy of CBT in treating various psychological disorders, particularly those characterized by negative thought patterns like depression and anxiety, the importance of this therapeutic approach becomes evident. By actively engaging in the process of cognitive change, individuals can experience a profound shift in their psychological well-being, underscoring the transformative power of CBT in fostering positive mental health outcomes.

CBT for thoughts related to life events

CBT is an evidence-based psychological treatment that aims to modify negative thought patterns, emotions, and behaviors. When it comes to thoughts related to life events, CBT offers targeted interventions that help individuals navigate and reframe their interpretations of past experiences. By utilizing techniques such as cognitive restructuring and problem-solving, individuals can challenge and change their automatic negative thoughts associated with various life events. For instance, if someone is persistently interpreting a past failure as a reflection of their incompetence, CBT can assist in reframing this thought to a more balanced and rational perspective. Through systematic exposure exercises and homework assignments, CBT helps individuals gradually confront and overcome their fears or negative associations related to life events, promoting resilience and adaptive coping strategies. Overall, CBT empowers individuals to restructure unhelpful thought patterns, leading to improved emotional well-being and enhanced coping skills in the face of life's challenges.

Effectiveness of CBT during transitional periods

During transitional periods, CBT has shown remarkable effectiveness in helping individuals navigate through changes by addressing negative thought patterns. This form of therapy, rooted in the cognitive model of psychopathology, emphasizes the interconnectedness of thoughts, emotions, and behaviors. By identifying and challenging irrational beliefs, CBT equips individuals with the tools to reframe their perceptions and responses to transitional stressors. Techniques like cognitive restructuring, problem-solving, and exposure are commonly utilized to modify negative thought patterns and promote adaptive coping strategies. Empirical evidence supports the efficacy of CBT in treating disorders like depression and anxiety, underscoring its ability to instigate positive cognitive shifts. Despite some criticisms, CBT's focus on restructuring maladaptive thinking remains a cornerstone in promoting psychological well-being during transitional phases, with implications for future research and therapeutic applications.

XXXVII. SPECIFIC POPULATIONS

In the realm of CBT, the application of this therapeutic approach to specific populations has shown promising results. Tailoring CBT techniques to address the unique needs of diverse groups, including children, adolescents, and older adults, is essential for optimizing treatment outcomes. For instance, adapting cognitive restructuring exercises to be more age-appropriate for children can enhance their engagement and comprehension. Similarly, integrating mindfulness practices into CBT for older adults can improve emotional regulation and coping skills. Moreover, CBT has been effective in treating individuals with comorbid conditions such as substance abuse and Post-Traumatic Stress Disorder (PTSD). By recognizing and accommodating the distinctive characteristics and challenges of each population, CBT can be a versatile and impactful tool in promoting positive cognitive and emotional changes across various demographics.

Tailoring CBT for the elderly

Tailoring CBT for the elderly presents a unique challenge due to the age-related cognitive and physical changes that can affect treatment outcomes. However, it is crucial to consider this population's specific needs to provide effective interventions. In adapting CBT for older adults, therapists must integrate techniques that address age-related issues, such as cognitive decline, chronic illness, and social isolation. Incorporating reminiscence therapy, behavioral activation, and relaxation exercises can enhance the effectiveness of CBT in this population. Furthermore, emphasizing practical strategies and simplifying cognitive restructuring exercises can improve comprehension and retention of skills. Tailored CBT interventions for the elderly not only target negative thought patterns but also promote overall well-being and quality of life. By recognizing and addressing the unique challenges faced by older adults, therapists can maximize the efficacy of CBT in this demographic and contribute to positive therapeutic outcomes.

CBT for veterans and trauma survivors

CBT has proven to be a highly effective approach in addressing negative thought patterns, particularly in populations such as veterans and trauma survivors who may experience intense and persistent negative emotions. By understanding the interplay between thoughts, emotions, and behaviors, CBT helps individuals identify and challenge distorted cognitions that contribute to their psychological distress. For veterans and trauma survivors, who may suffer from conditions like PTSD, anxiety, and depression, CBT offers tangible techniques like cognitive restructuring and exposure therapy to reframe their perceptions and confront their fears. Research studies have consistently shown the efficacy of CBT in treating these specific disorders by targeting negative thought patterns directly. Despite some criticisms and limitations, the empirical evidence highlights the significant impact of CBT on improving psychological well-being and fostering resilience in individuals facing trauma-related challenges. As we look to the future, further research and clinical applications of CBT hold promises for enhancing the mental health outcomes of those who have experienced traumatic events.

Adapting CBT for individuals with disabilities

Adapting CBT for individuals with disabilities requires a nuanced approach that considers the unique challenges they may face. Incorporating principles of CBT into therapy for individuals with disabilities can be highly beneficial in addressing negative thought patterns and promoting emotional well-being. By adapting traditional CBT techniques to suit the specific needs of these individuals, therapists can help them recognize and challenge their negative thoughts effectively. For instance, using accessible language, incorporating visual aids, or employing alternative communication methods can enhance the therapeutic process for individuals with disabilities. Additionally, focusing on building coping strategies tailored to their specific circumstances can empower these individuals to manage their emotions more effectively. Ultimately, adapting CBT for individuals with disabilities underscores the importance of inclusivity in mental health care and strives to improve their overall quality of life through targeted psychological interventions.

XXXVIII. COMORBID CONDITIONS

CBT is a widely recognized therapeutic approach that aims to modify negative thought patterns, behaviors, and emotions. When addressing comorbid conditions, such as depression and anxiety, CBT becomes a valuable tool in treatment. By targeting specific negative thought patterns associated with each disorder, CBT can effectively address the interconnected nature of comorbid conditions. For instance, in treating both depression and anxiety simultaneously, CBT helps individuals recognize and challenge maladaptive thoughts, leading to a reduction in symptoms associated with both disorders. The ability of CBT to address multiple conditions concurrently showcases its versatility and effectiveness in clinical practice. By tailoring interventions to target comorbid conditions and their unique thought patterns, CBT offers a comprehensive approach to managing complex psychological presentations. Through structured techniques like cognitive restructuring and exposure therapy, CBT equips individuals with the skills needed to navigate the challenges posed by comorbidity, ultimately promoting better mental health outcomes.

Addressing multiple disorders with CBT

CBT is a widely utilized therapeutic approach in clinical psychology that focuses on altering negative thought patterns to improve overall mental health. When individuals present with multiple disorders, CBT offers a comprehensive method to address these interconnected issues. By targeting cognitive distortions and maladaptive behaviors, CBT helps individuals understand the relationship between their thoughts, emotions, and actions. Through cognitive restructuring, problem-solving techniques, and exposure exercises, therapists guide clients in challenging and modifying their negative beliefs and behaviors. This approach not only fosters greater self-awareness but also empowers individuals to make lasting changes in their thought processes. Research indicates the effectiveness of CBT in treating various disorders such as depression and anxiety by specifically targeting negative thought patterns. By incorporating CBT techniques into therapeutic interventions, clinicians can provide holistic and tailored treatment plans for individuals struggling with multiple disorders, ultimately promoting long-term psychological well-being. A deeper exploration of CBT's efficacy in addressing comorbid conditions could offer valuable insights for future research and practice in the field of clinical psychology.

Integrative approaches within CBT

Integrative approaches within CBT have gained recognition for their ability to enhance the effectiveness of traditional CBT methods. These approaches involve blending CBT techniques with elements from other therapeutic modalities, such as mindfulness-based interventions, ACT, or psychodynamic therapy. By integrating these diverse techniques, therapists can tailor their interventions to the specific needs of each client, leading to more personalized and comprehensive treatment outcomes. Research has shown that integrative approaches within CBT can significantly improve treatment outcomes, particularly for complex issues like comorbid conditions or treatment-resistant cases. By combining the strengths of different therapeutic modalities, integrative approaches within CBT offer a more nuanced and versatile approach to addressing negative thought patterns, highlighting the importance of individualized and multimodal interventions in the field of clinical psychology.

Outcomes for comorbid conditions

Comorbid conditions, which often accompany psychological disorders, can significantly influence the outcomes of CBT. Research has shown that individuals with comorbid conditions may have more complex symptom presentations and treatment needs, leading to potentially less favorable outcomes in traditional CBT interventions. It is essential for clinicians to consider these comorbidities when designing treatment plans, as addressing multiple conditions simultaneously can be challenging. Tailoring CBT techniques to address the specific needs and challenges presented by comorbid conditions is crucial for successful outcomes. By incorporating strategies to manage co-occurring disorders effectively, such as integrated treatment approaches or modifications to standard CBT protocols, therapists can enhance the efficacy of interventions and improve overall patient well-being. Ultimately, understanding the impact of comorbid conditions on CBT outcomes is essential for providing comprehensive and effective care to individuals with complex psychological needs.

XXXIX. SUPERVISION AND CONSULTATION

Supervision and consultation play crucial roles in ensuring the effective implementation of CBT in clinical practice. Supervision provides a platform for therapists to receive guidance, feedback, and support in dealing with complex cases or challenging clients. Through supervision, therapists can enhance their skills, gain insights into their clinical work, and ensure adherence to CBT principles and techniques. Consultation, on the other hand, offers an opportunity for therapists to collaborate with their peers, share experiences, and seek advice on difficult cases. The interchange of ideas and perspectives in consultations can enrich therapeutic interventions and provide a broader understanding of CBT applications. Both supervision and consultation contribute to the ongoing professional development of therapists, ultimately improving the quality of care and outcomes for clients undergoing treatment for negative thought patterns within the realm of CBT.

The role of supervision in therapist development

Supervision plays a crucial role in the development of therapists within the framework of CBT. Through regular supervision sessions, therapists receive guidance, feedback, and support from experienced supervisors, which aids in enhancing their clinical skills and confidence. Supervision serves as a reflective space where therapists can explore and address any challenges they encounter while working with clients, especially when attempting to modify negative thought patterns. These sessions provide an opportunity for therapists to receive constructive criticism, learn new techniques, and deepen their understanding of the theoretical underpinnings of CBT. Moreover, supervision fosters a culture of continuous learning and professional development, ultimately contributing to the quality of patient care and the therapist's overall competence in implementing effective interventions to change negative thought patterns. In summary, supervision acts as a cornerstone in therapist development, facilitating the successful application of CBT principles in clinical practice.

Models of consultation for CBT practitioners

Models of consultation for CBT practitioners play a crucial role in enhancing the effectiveness of cognitive-behavioral therapy interventions. Consultation models like peer consultation, expert consultation, and group consultation offer CBT practitioners a platform to discuss challenging cases, explore new techniques, and receive feedback on their clinical work. Peer consultation, for instance, facilitates collaboration among colleagues, fostering a sense of community and providing opportunities for mutual learning. Expert consultation allows practitioners to seek guidance from seasoned professionals, gaining insights from their wealth of experience. Group consultation, on the other hand, encourages brainstorming and diverse perspectives, enriching the therapeutic process. By engaging in these consultation models, CBT practitioners can refine their skills, stay updated on the latest research, and ultimately deliver more comprehensive and tailored interventions for clients with negative thought patterns. Therefore, incorporating varied consultation models into CBT practice is essential for promoting continuous professional growth and improving therapeutic outcomes.

Impact of supervision on therapy outcomes

Supervision in therapy plays a crucial role in shaping therapy outcomes. Effective supervision enhances therapist competence and adherence to treatment protocols, ultimately influencing the effectiveness of the therapy provided. The impact of supervision on therapy outcomes can be seen in various ways. Primarily, it ensures that therapists receive ongoing support, guidance, and feedback to address any challenges they encounter during therapy sessions. This, in turn, leads to improved therapist confidence and the delivery of evidence-based interventions. Additionally, supervision allows for the monitoring of progress and the identification of areas for improvement, thus facilitating better client outcomes. Ultimately, a well-structured and supportive supervision system contributes significantly to the success of therapy interventions by promoting therapist growth and skill development, which directly impacts the quality of care provided to clients.

XL. TRAINING PROGRAMS AND CERTIFICATION

CBT training programs and certification play a pivotal role in ensuring the competency and effectiveness of practitioners in implementing Cognitive Behavioral Therapy techniques. These programs typically encompass a thorough understanding of the theoretical foundations of CBT, the interplay between thoughts, emotions, and behaviors, as well as the application of specific methods and techniques for modifying negative thought patterns. Certification in CBT signifies a clinician's proficiency in utilizing cognitive restructuring, problem-solving, and exposure therapies to bring about positive cognitive and behavioral changes in clients. Research studies showcasing the empirical evidence supporting the efficacy of CBT in treating various disorders, particularly those rooted in negative thought patterns like depression and anxiety, further emphasize the significance of quality training and certification programs for mental health professionals. As such, investing in comprehensive CBT training and certification not only enhances practitioners' skills but also ensures high-quality care for individuals struggling with negative thought patterns.

Accreditation and certification processes

Accreditation and certification processes play a vital role in ensuring the quality and effectiveness of CBT interventions aimed at changing negative thought patterns. Accreditation serves as a stamp of approval, indicating that a particular CBT program meets high standards of training, supervision, and ethical practice. Certification, on the other hand, demonstrates that individual therapists have undergone rigorous training and assessment to deliver CBT competently. These processes not only enhance the credibility of CBT but also protect clients from potential harm caused by unqualified practitioners. By adhering to accredited programs and seeking certified therapists, individuals can trust in the efficacy and safety of CBT interventions designed to modify negative thought patterns. Ultimately, accreditation and certification processes uphold the professionalism and integrity of CBT as a cornerstone in the field of clinical psychology.

Curriculum and competencies for CBT training

In defining the curriculum and competencies for CBT training, it is crucial to consider the foundational knowledge and skills required for therapists to effectively change negative thought patterns in their clients. The training should encompass a comprehensive understanding of the cognitive model of psychopathology, which forms the basis of CBT interventions. Therapists must be proficient in identifying maladaptive thought processes, restructuring cognitive distortions, and implementing behavioral interventions to address negative patterns effectively. Additionally, competence in establishing and maintaining a therapeutic alliance, conducting thorough assessments, and evaluating treatment progress is essential for successful CBT outcomes. Training programs should include supervised practice, feedback mechanisms, and ongoing professional development opportunities to ensure therapists receive the necessary support and guidance to apply CBT competencies effectively in clinical practice. This focused training approach is vital in equipping therapists with the tools and skills needed to help individuals overcome negative thought patterns and improve psychological well-being through CBT interventions.

Continuing education and professional development

Continuing education and professional development play a crucial role in mastering the intricacies of CBT and effectively changing negative thought patterns. By engaging in ongoing education, therapists can stay abreast of the latest research, interventions, and best practices in the field. This continuous learning empowers clinicians to refine their skills, gain new perspectives, and adapt to evolving client needs. Furthermore, professional development opportunities provide a platform for networking, collaboration, and mentorship within the CBT community. Through workshops, conferences, and supervision sessions, therapists can receive constructive feedback, learn from peers, and enhance their therapeutic abilities. By investing in continued education, clinicians not only elevate their own practice but also contribute to the advancement and efficacy of CBT as a therapeutic modality in addressing negative thought patterns.

XLI. NON-CLINICAL SETTINGS

CBT has traditionally been associated with clinical settings, where it is utilized to treat various psychological disorders by targeting negative thought patterns. However, the application of CBT in non-clinical settings has gained recognition for its efficacy in enhancing individual well-being and performance. By incorporating CBT techniques such as cognitive restructuring and problem-solving into non-clinical environments, individuals can develop skills to manage stress, improve decision-making, and enhance overall mental resilience. This shift towards utilizing CBT in non-clinical settings highlights the versatility and effectiveness of this therapeutic approach beyond traditional clinical applications. As more research emerges on the benefits of CBT in non-traditional contexts, it becomes increasingly apparent that this intervention has the potential to positively impact a wide range of individuals seeking to improve their cognitive and emotional well-being outside of formal therapy settings.

Preventive applications of CBT

Preventive applications of CBT are vital in addressing negative thought patterns before they escalate into more severe mental health issues. By focusing on early intervention and teaching individuals skills to challenge and reframe their negative thoughts, CBT can be an effective tool in preventing the development of conditions such as anxiety and depression. Through techniques like cognitive restructuring and problem-solving, individuals can learn to identify and replace maladaptive thoughts with more realistic and positive ones. The emphasis on changing thought patterns in a preventive way not only promotes mental well-being but also equips individuals with lifelong coping mechanisms. By implementing CBT in a preventive context, clinicians can empower individuals to break the cycle of negativity and cultivate a more resilient mindset, ultimately leading to improved psychological health and overall quality of life.

CBT in schools and educational settings

CBT in schools and educational settings offers a promising avenue for addressing negative thought patterns in adolescents. By introducing cognitive-behavioral interventions in educational curricula, students can learn valuable tools for managing stress, anxiety, and other psychological challenges. These interventions typically focus on teaching students how to identify and challenge their negative thoughts, reframe unhelpful beliefs, and develop effective coping strategies. By equipping young individuals with these cognitive-behavioral skills early on, educators can help prevent the development of more severe mental health issues later in life. Research has shown the effectiveness of CBT in school settings, with improvements in academic performance, emotional regulation, and overall well-being. However, challenges such as limited resources and training for educators must be addressed to ensure the successful implementation of CBT programs in schools. Overall, integrating CBT into educational settings holds great potential for creating a supportive environment that fosters positive mental health outcomes in students.

Community-based CBT programs

Community-based CBT programs are an essential component of mental health care delivery, offering accessible and effective treatment for individuals struggling with negative thought patterns. By engaging with communities, these programs can reach a broader spectrum of individuals who may not have access to traditional therapy settings. Community-based CBT programs often involve group therapy sessions that provide a supportive environment for individuals to challenge and reframe their negative thoughts. These programs also incorporate elements of psychoeducation, helping participants develop a deeper understanding of their thought patterns and behaviors. By fostering a sense of belonging and collaboration, community-based CBT programs empower individuals to actively participate in their own therapeutic journey. Furthermore, these programs have been shown to be cost-effective and sustainable, making them a valuable resource in addressing mental health challenges at a grassroots level. Overall, community-based CBT programs play a vital role in enhancing the psychological well-being of individuals by promoting the identification and modification of negative thought patterns within a supportive community setting.

XLII. THE BIOPSYCHOSOCIAL MODEL

CBT, grounded in the biopsychosocial model, offers a comprehensive approach to modifying negative thought patterns. By understanding how biological, psychological, and social factors interact in influencing mental health, CBT practitioners can tailor interventions to address the root causes of distorted thinking. This model acknowledges that negative thoughts are not solely the result of internal cognitive processes but are shaped by external experiences and societal influences. In practice, CBT therapists employ cognitive restructuring techniques to challenge and reframe maladaptive beliefs, while also incorporating behavioral interventions to encourage positive changes in actions and emotions. This multifaceted approach ensures a holistic transformation of individuals' thought patterns, enhancing their overall well-being. By integrating the biopsychosocial model into CBT, therapists can effectively target and modify negative thought patterns, leading to lasting, positive outcomes for clients.

Integrating biological factors in CBT

Integrating biological factors in CBT can enhance the effectiveness of treatment for individuals with negative thought patterns. By considering the biological underpinnings of mental health issues, such as genetic predispositions, neurotransmitter imbalances, and neurological abnormalities, therapists can personalize CBT interventions to target these specific factors. For instance, incorporating techniques like mindfulness meditation or physical exercise can modulate brain activity and promote positive cognitive restructuring. By combining psychological strategies with biological interventions, CBT can address the root causes of negative thought patterns and provide a more holistic approach to mental healthcare. This integrative approach not only improves symptom management but also fosters long-term resilience and emotional well-being. Overall, incorporating biological factors in CBT underscores the importance of a comprehensive understanding of individual experiences and challenges in the treatment process.

The psychological and social dimensions in CBT

In CBT, the psychological and social dimensions play crucial roles in the process of changing negative thought patterns. The cognitive model of psychopathology underpinning CBT emphasizes the interrelation between thoughts, emotions, and behaviors, highlighting the significance of addressing both inner cognitive processes and external social factors. By identifying and challenging maladaptive thought patterns through cognitive restructuring, individuals can effectively modify their cognitive distortions and negative beliefs. Moreover, CBT incorporates social learning principles, such as exposure therapy and problem-solving techniques, to help individuals navigate real-world scenarios that trigger negative thoughts. The collaborative nature of the therapeutic relationship in CBT also fosters social support and enhances self-efficacy, empowering individuals to challenge their negative thought patterns effectively. Overall, the integration of psychological and social dimensions in CBT contributes to its efficacy in promoting lasting changes in individuals' cognitive patterns and overall well-being.

Holistic approaches within the CBT framework

Within the CBT framework, holistic approaches play a vital role in addressing negative thought patterns. Unlike traditional therapies that focus solely on symptoms, CBT considers the individual as a whole, incorporating cognitive, emotional, behavioral, and physiological aspects into treatment. By adopting a holistic perspective, therapists can better understand the interconnected nature of thoughts, emotions, and behaviors, leading to more comprehensive interventions. Through techniques like cognitive restructuring, problem-solving, and exposure therapy, CBT aims to target not only the surface-level negative thoughts but also the underlying beliefs and cognitive distortions that fuel them. This integrated approach allows individuals to gain a deeper insight into their thought patterns and develop more adaptive coping strategies. By addressing the root causes of negative thinking, CBT empowers individuals to make lasting changes that promote overall psychological well-being. Thus, embracing holistic approaches within the CBT framework can enhance the effectiveness of therapy in transforming negative thought patterns and fostering positive growth.

XLIII. HEALTH PSYCHOLOGY

CBT in the context of health psychology, particularly in modifying negative thought patterns, plays a crucial role in improving overall well-being. With its roots in the cognitive revolution of the 1960s, CBT emphasizes the interplay between thoughts, emotions, and behaviors. By targeting maladaptive schemas and cognitive distortions, CBT aims to reframe negative thought patterns and promote more adaptive ways of thinking. By utilizing techniques such as cognitive restructuring, problem-solving, and exposure therapy, individuals can effectively challenge and change their negative cognitions. The empirical evidence supporting the efficacy of CBT in treating various mental health disorders, including anxiety and depression, further underscores its significance in promoting positive psychological outcomes. While criticisms and limitations exist, particularly in terms of individual differences and treatment adherence, CBT remains a powerful tool in addressing and transforming negative thought patterns for improved health and well-being.

CBT for health behavior change

CBT is a widely recognized approach in clinical psychology, specifically targeted at altering negative thought patterns and their associated behaviors. Developed by prominent figures like Aaron Beck and Albert Ellis, CBT operates on the premise that thoughts, emotions, and behaviors are interrelated, with changing one component influencing the others. Through techniques such as cognitive restructuring, problem-solving, and exposure, CBT aims to help individuals identify and challenge their negative beliefs, ultimately leading to more adaptive thought patterns. Research studies have consistently demonstrated the effectiveness of CBT in treating various disorders, particularly depression and anxiety, by focusing on modifying these maladaptive thinking processes. While CBT has shown significant success, it is essential to acknowledge its limitations and consider alternative therapeutic approaches to negative thought patterns. Overall, the emphasis on changing negative thought patterns in CBT reflects the critical role of cognitive processes in shaping psychological well-being, highlighting the importance of ongoing research and development in this field.

Cognitive interventions for chronic illness

Cognitive interventions for chronic illness play a vital role in the management and treatment of these conditions, as they address not only the physical symptoms but also the psychological aspects that often accompany chronic illness. CBT is a particularly effective approach in this regard, aiming to change negative thought patterns that can exacerbate the experience of living with a chronic illness. By identifying and challenging maladaptive beliefs and behaviors, individuals undergoing CBT can develop more adaptive coping strategies and improve their overall quality of life. Through techniques such as cognitive restructuring and problem-solving, individuals can learn to reframe their perspectives and manage stress more effectively. The application of CBT in chronic illness management highlights the crucial link between psychological well-being and physical health, emphasizing the need for integrated interventions that address both aspects of an individual's health.

The role of CBT in health promotion

CBT plays a pivotal role in health promotion by targeting negative thought patterns and promoting positive cognitive restructuring. Through the examination of the interplay between thoughts, emotions, and behaviors, CBT provides individuals with the tools to identify and challenge maladaptive beliefs, leading to a shift towards healthier thinking patterns. Techniques such as cognitive restructuring, problem-solving, and exposure therapy are integral to the process of altering negative thought patterns. Research studies have consistently demonstrated the effectiveness of CBT in treating various mental health disorders, particularly depression and anxiety, by addressing the underlying cognitive distortions contributing to these conditions. By empowering individuals to recognize and modify their negative thought patterns, CBT not only improves symptom management but also enhances overall psychological well-being. As such, the utilization of CBT in health promotion endeavors holds significant promise for fostering lasting positive change in individuals' mental health.

XLIV. SPIRITUALITY

CBT, as a highly effective therapeutic approach in clinical psychology, aims to modify negative thought patterns that contribute to various psychological disorders. By examining the interplay between thoughts, emotions, and behaviors, CBT targets these maladaptive cognitions through techniques like cognitive restructuring and problem-solving. However, an often-overlooked aspect of CBT is its relationship with spirituality. Incorporating spirituality into CBT can provide profound benefits for individuals seeking to change negative thought patterns. By tapping into individuals' deeper beliefs and values, CBT can help them find meaning, purpose, and inner peace. This holistic approach acknowledges the interconnectedness of mental, emotional, and spiritual well-being. Future research should explore the integration of spirituality into CBT more deeply to enhance its therapeutic efficacy and address the existential dimensions of human experience. Through this synergistic relationship, CBT can further empower individuals in their journey towards positive psychological transformation.

Addressing spiritual beliefs in CBT

It could be a pivotal aspect in enhancing the effectiveness of therapy, especially when dealing with negative thought patterns. Incorporating spiritual beliefs into CBT can provide individuals with a deeper sense of purpose, hope, and resilience. By acknowledging and integrating these beliefs, therapists can create a more holistic approach to treatment that resonates with the client's values and worldview. Additionally, addressing spiritual beliefs can foster a sense of connection and meaning, which can counteract feelings of isolation and distress commonly associated with negative thinking. Embracing spirituality in therapy can empower individuals to draw strength from their faith or beliefs, ultimately aiding in the transformation of negative thought patterns into more positive and adaptive ones. This inclusive approach recognizes the multifaceted nature of human experience and highlights the importance of addressing all aspects of an individual's identity in the therapeutic process.

The impact of spirituality on thought patterns

The impact of spirituality on thought patterns is a multifaceted concept that can significantly influence an individual's cognitive functioning. Spirituality, often linked to beliefs in a higher power or purpose, can provide a framework for understanding and interpreting life events, shaping thoughts, emotions, and behaviors. In the context of CBT, incorporating spiritual beliefs can offer clients alternative perspectives on their negative thought patterns. By integrating spiritual practices such as mindfulness, meditation, or prayer, individuals may develop a more positive outlook, challenge distorted thinking, and cultivate resilience in the face of adversity. This integration expands the therapeutic toolkit, allowing clinicians to address the spiritual dimensions of their clients' lives and promote holistic healing. Ultimately, the blending of spirituality with CBT can enhance interventions, foster personal growth, and contribute to more profound transformations in thought patterns, ultimately improving overall psychological well-being.

Research on CBT and spiritual well-being

Research on CBT and spiritual well-being has gained attention in recent years, as mental health professionals explore holistic approaches to psychological treatment. While CBT traditionally focuses on changing negative thought patterns through structured cognitive restructuring techniques, some studies have delved into the intersection of CBT with spiritual practices to enhance well-being. Research suggests that incorporating spiritual elements into CBT can lead to more profound and lasting changes in individuals' thought patterns, emotions, and behaviors. By integrating mindfulness, meditation, or existential themes into CBT interventions, therapists can address not only surface-level negative thoughts but also underlying existential or spiritual concerns that may contribute to psychological distress. This approach can offer a more comprehensive and personalized therapeutic experience, acknowledging the interconnectedness of individuals' cognitive, emotional, and spiritual facets in promoting overall well-being. Further exploration of the synergies between CBT and spiritual practices could enrich therapeutic outcomes and potentially expand the scope of CBT in addressing various mental health challenges.

XLV. POSITIVE PSYCHOLOGY

CBT has emerged as a prominent therapeutic approach in clinical psychology due to its efficacy in changing negative thought patterns. Developed by pioneers like Aaron Beck and Albert Ellis, CBT is rooted in the cognitive model of psychopathology, which highlights the interconnectedness of thoughts, emotions, and behaviors. Through techniques such as cognitive restructuring, problem-solving, and exposure, CBT helps individuals identify and modify maladaptive beliefs that contribute to negative thinking. Empirical evidence supports the effectiveness of CBT in treating disorders like depression and anxiety by targeting these cognitive distortions. While some critics point out limitations, CBT remains a cornerstone in mental health treatment. Its focus on altering negative thought patterns not only alleviates symptoms but also promotes overall psychological well-being. As research in this field continues to expand, the potential applications of CBT for diverse populations and settings offer promising avenues for future exploration.

Incorporating strengths-based approaches

Incorporating strengths-based approaches within CBT is an innovative way to enhance the effectiveness of therapy sessions. By focusing on identifying and leveraging the individual's strengths, therapists can empower clients to challenge and change their negative thought patterns more effectively. This approach not only helps in building self-esteem and resilience but also facilitates quicker progress in therapy by tapping into existing resources. Strengths-based CBT encourages a positive and collaborative therapeutic relationship, where clients feel validated and supported in their journey towards overcoming negative cognitive patterns. Utilizing strengths-based approaches within the framework of CBT allows for a more holistic and empowering therapeutic experience, setting the stage for lasting change and improved psychological well-being. By celebrating and utilizing strengths, individuals can navigate their challenges with newfound confidence and self-awareness, making the process of changing negative thought patterns more manageable and sustainable in the long run.

The enhancement of well-being

CBT plays a crucial role in enhancing well-being by targeting negative thought patterns at their core. Through the process of cognitive restructuring, individuals are guided to identify and challenge maladaptive beliefs, leading to a shift in cognition that positively influences emotions and behaviors. This approach, rooted in the cognitive model of psychopathology, emphasizes the interconnectedness of thoughts, feelings, and actions. By addressing distorted thinking patterns and replacing them with more rational and adaptive ones, CBT equips individuals with the tools to manage stress, improve mood, and foster resilience. Empirical evidence supports the effectiveness of CBT in treating various psychological disorders, particularly depression and anxiety, by facilitating lasting changes in thought patterns. Ultimately, the profound impact of CBT on well-being underscores its significance in promoting mental health and overall psychological flourishing. The exploration of further applications and research in this therapeutic approach holds promising prospects for continued advancements in cognitive and emotional well-being.

Positive CBT interventions and outcomes

Positive CBT interventions and outcomes play a crucial role in the process of changing negative thought patterns. By utilizing cognitive restructuring, problem-solving techniques, and exposure exercises, CBT therapists can help individuals challenge and modify their maladaptive beliefs and behaviors. These interventions aim to break the cycle of negative thinking, reduce distress, and improve overall well-being. Through empirical evidence, it has been established that CBT is effective in treating various mental health conditions, including depression and anxiety, by targeting negative thought patterns at their core. While some critics may point out limitations of CBT, such as its focus on cognitive processes over emotional aspects, the positive outcomes observed in clinical practice cannot be denied. Overall, CBT interventions offer a structured and evidence-based approach to fostering more adaptive and positive thought patterns, leading to significant improvements in psychological functioning and quality of life. As research in this field continues to grow, further exploration of nuanced applications and tailored interventions within CBT holds promise for addressing a wider range of mental health concerns.

XLVI. THE THERAPEUTIC PROCESS

CBT, an essential tool in clinical psychology, is focused on changing negative thought patterns to promote better mental health. The therapeutic process in CBT involves a collaborative effort between the therapist and the individual seeking help. Initially, cognitive restructuring is employed to challenge and reframe irrational beliefs that contribute to negative thinking. By identifying and addressing these maladaptive thought patterns, individuals can learn to substitute them with more positive and realistic cognitions. Through the use of problem-solving techniques and exposure exercises, clients can confront their fears and anxieties in a controlled manner, gradually modifying their responses. The empirical evidence supporting CBT's effectiveness in treating various disorders, such as depression and anxiety, highlights its efficacy in changing negative thought patterns. While criticisms exist, the impact of CBT on psychological well-being is undeniable, emphasizing the importance of continued research and application in this therapeutic approach.

Stages of CBT and therapeutic progression

In the stages of CBT, therapeutic progression follows a systematic approach aimed at changing negative thought patterns. Initially, the therapist and client establish a collaborative relationship, setting goals and outlining the framework for treatment. The cognitive restructuring phase comes next, where dysfunctional beliefs and negative thoughts are identified and challenged. Techniques such as thought records and Socratic questioning are utilized to modify these maladaptive thought patterns. Subsequently, behavioral experiments are conducted to test the validity of these new beliefs in real-world situations. As the therapy progresses, clients learn to apply these cognitive-behavioral skills independently, leading to a decrease in negative thinking and improvement in overall well-being. The gradual progression through these stages is crucial for the successful transformation of negative thought patterns, demonstrating the effectiveness of CBT in promoting positive change in individuals.

Therapist adaptability and client responsiveness

Therapist adaptability and client responsiveness play pivotal roles in the successful application of CBT to change negative thought patterns. Therapist adaptability refers to the ability of the therapist to tailor therapeutic interventions to meet the unique needs and challenges of each individual client. By adapting their approach based on the client's personality, beliefs, and readiness to change, therapists can create a more effective therapeutic alliance. This, in turn, enhances client responsiveness, whereby individuals actively engage in the therapeutic process and are more receptive to exploring and modifying their negative thought patterns. When therapists demonstrate flexibility and sensitivity in their interventions, clients are more likely to trust and collaborate with them, leading to more profound and lasting changes in cognition, emotion, and behavior. Therefore, the dynamic interplay between therapist adaptability and client responsiveness is crucial for the successful implementation of CBT in addressing negative thought patterns.

Process research in CBT

Process research in CBT plays a crucial role in understanding how individuals modify their negative thought patterns. Through meticulous observation and analysis, researchers have identified key processes involved in cognitive restructuring, a core technique in CBT. By examining how individuals interact with their maladaptive thoughts, emotions, and behaviors, process researchers uncover the underlying mechanisms that drive effective change in cognitive patterns. These studies highlight the importance of cognitive flexibility, problem-solving skills, and exposure to challenging situations in breaking the cycle of negative thinking. By elucidating the intricate processes involved in CBT, researchers provide valuable insights into the therapeutic mechanisms that underpin the success of this approach. Ultimately, process research in CBT contributes to enhancing the effectiveness and refinement of interventions aimed at altering negative thought patterns, leading to improved psychological well-being for individuals seeking relief from distressing cognitive patterns.

XLVII. PERSONAL GROWTH

CBT stands out as a powerful tool in the realm of psychology, particularly when it comes to fostering personal growth. By delving into the intricate interplay between thoughts, emotions, and behaviors, CBT offers individuals the opportunity to identify and modify negative thought patterns that may be hindering their progress. Through techniques like cognitive restructuring, problem-solving, and exposure, individuals can gain a deeper understanding of their cognitive processes and learn to challenge and reframe unhelpful beliefs. The transformative potential of CBT lies in its ability to empower individuals to take control of their thoughts and emotions, ultimately leading to enhanced psychological well-being. As research continues to support the efficacy of CBT in various mental health conditions, the significance of addressing and changing negative thought patterns for personal growth becomes increasingly evident. However, further research and exploration are essential to unlock the full potential of CBT in facilitating lasting personal growth and development.

CBT's contribution to self-improvement

CBT stands as a pivotal approach in clinical psychology, emphasizing the modification of negative thought patterns to promote self-improvement. Grounded in the cognitive model of psychopathology, CBT operates on the principle that thoughts, emotions, and behaviors are interconnected, influencing one another. Through techniques like cognitive restructuring and problem-solving, individuals are empowered to challenge and change their maladaptive thought patterns. By identifying and replacing distorted beliefs with more realistic interpretations, CBT assists in fostering healthier cognitions and promoting positive behavioral changes. Empirical evidence underscores the efficacy of CBT in treating various mental health conditions, particularly depression and anxiety. This strategic intervention not only addresses immediate concerns but also equips individuals with enduring coping skills that contribute to their overall psychological well-being. Looking ahead, continued research and application of CBT hold promise for further advancements in the realm of self-improvement and mental health.

Cognitive approaches to personal development

Cognitive approaches to personal development, particularly within the framework of CBT, offer a structured and evidence-based method for changing negative thought patterns. Grounded in the belief that our thoughts influence our emotions and behaviors, CBT focuses on understanding and challenging distorted cognitions to promote healthier psychological functioning. By identifying and altering cognitive distortions through techniques such as cognitive restructuring and problem-solving, individuals can reframe their beliefs and perceptions, leading to positive behavioral changes and emotional well-being. This cognitive restructuring process is guided by a collaborative therapeutic relationship, where the therapist and client work together to examine and challenge negative thought patterns. Through empirical research demonstrating the efficacy of CBT in treating various mental health conditions, including depression and anxiety, the cognitive approach has gained widespread recognition for its effectiveness in aiding personal development by reshaping maladaptive cognitive processes towards more adaptive and constructive thinking patterns.

Case studies on personal growth through CBT

Case studies showcasing personal growth through the application of CBT provide valuable insights into the transformative potential of this therapeutic approach. Individuals participating in CBT sessions work with trained therapists to identify and challenge negative thought patterns, leading to significant improvements in emotional well-being. For instance, a study on individuals struggling with anxiety disorders revealed that cognitive restructuring techniques in CBT helped participants recognize and modify their erroneous thinking, resulting in decreased anxiety levels and increased self-confidence. These findings underscore the efficacy of CBT in facilitating personal growth by empowering individuals to break free from maladaptive thinking patterns and embrace more positive and adaptive beliefs. Through structured sessions and targeted interventions, CBT serves as a catalyst for profound psychological changes, paving the way for enhanced mental health and well-being.

XLVIII. FAMILY SYSTEMS

CBT has long been recognized for its effectiveness in addressing negative thought patterns, but its application within family systems brings a new dimension to therapy. By considering not only the individual but also the dynamics of the family unit, CBT can target ingrained patterns of thinking that may have originated or been perpetuated within familial relationships. Understanding the interplay between family members and how their thoughts, emotions, and behaviors interact can provide valuable insights for CBT practitioners seeking to enact meaningful change. Through exploring family dynamics and communication patterns, CBT can unearth and challenge core beliefs, fostering a deeper understanding of how negative thought patterns are reinforced within the family system. By integrating family systems theory with CBT techniques, therapists can offer holistic and tailored interventions that address not only individual cognitions but also the broader relational context in which negative thought patterns may persist. This integration underscores the importance of considering familial influences when working towards cognitive restructuring and emotional regulation, illustrating the depth and breadth of CBT's capabilities in transforming negative thought patterns within a systemic framework.

The intersection of CBT and family therapy

The intersection of CBT and family therapy presents a multifaceted approach to addressing negative thought patterns within the context of familial relationships. While CBT focuses on changing individual cognitive distortions, family therapy highlights the impact of family dynamics on an individual's mental health. By integrating these two therapeutic modalities, therapists can examine how family interactions contribute to the development and maintenance of negative thought patterns. Through collaborative sessions with both the individual and their family members, CBT techniques such as cognitive restructuring and behavioral activation can be adapted to address relational patterns that perpetuate negative thinking. This integrated approach not only enhances the effectiveness of treatment but also provides a holistic understanding of the interconnectedness between individual cognition and familial influences in shaping thought patterns. By recognizing and modifying these dynamics, individuals can experience lasting change and improved mental well-being.

Addressing family dynamics and thought patterns

Addressing family dynamics and thought patterns within the context of CBT is crucial for successful treatment outcomes. Families often play a significant role in shaping an individual's thought patterns and cognitive distortions. By exploring familial relationships and communication styles, therapists can identify the underlying triggers for negative thoughts and behaviors. CBT techniques aim to challenge and reframe these distortions through collaboration with the individual and, when appropriate, their family members. By addressing dysfunctional thought patterns within the family system, CBT can evoke lasting changes by promoting healthier communication, problem-solving skills, and emotional regulation. Moreover, integrating family dynamics into CBT can enhance the individual's understanding of how their thoughts are influenced by their environment, leading to more sustainable positive changes in cognition and behavior. This holistic approach underscores the importance of considering family dynamics in the therapeutic process for addressing negative thought patterns effectively.

Outcomes of CBT in family contexts

CBT has shown significant positive outcomes when applied in family contexts. By addressing negative thought patterns within the family unit, CBT can improve overall communication, foster healthier relationships, and enhance problem-solving skills. When family members engage in cognitive restructuring techniques together, they can challenge and modify dysfunctional beliefs that may have been perpetuated over time. By encouraging open dialogue and teaching effective coping strategies, CBT can help families navigate conflicts and stressors more constructively. Research suggests that involving the entire family in therapy can lead to better treatment outcomes, particularly in cases of depression, anxiety, or behavioral issues. Moreover, the skills acquired through CBT in a family setting can extend beyond therapy sessions, enabling lasting positive changes that contribute to overall psychological well-being for all members involved. This family-focused approach highlights the powerful impact that CBT can have on interpersonal dynamics and individual mental health within a familial context.

XLIX. COUPLE THERAPY

In the context of couple therapy, CBT plays a vital role in addressing negative thought patterns that may hinder relationship dynamics. By delving into individuals' cognitive distortions and maladaptive beliefs within the relationship framework, CBT can effectively facilitate communication and understanding between partners. Through the identification of negative thought patterns, such as irrational beliefs or catastrophic thinking, couples can learn to challenge and reframe these distortions, leading to improved conflict resolution and emotional regulation. Moreover, CBT techniques, such as cognitive restructuring and behavioral experiments, can help couples develop healthier communication styles and coping mechanisms, ultimately fostering a more harmonious and fulfilling relationship. By integrating CBT principles into couple therapy, clinicians can empower partners to navigate challenges, enhance empathy, and cultivate a supportive and resilient bond based on mutual understanding and adaptive coping mechanisms.

CBT techniques for relationship issues

CBT offers a variety of techniques to address relationship issues by modifying negative thought patterns. Initially developed by Aaron Beck and Albert Ellis, CBT focuses on identifying and challenging irrational thoughts that contribute to distressing emotions and maladaptive behaviors. One key technique in CBT is cognitive restructuring, which helps individuals recognize, challenge, and replace negative thought patterns with more balanced and adaptive ones. Through guided exercises, individuals can reframe their beliefs about themselves, their partners, and their relationships, leading to improved communication, problem-solving, and coping strategies. Additionally, CBT encompasses techniques like problem-solving skills training and exposure therapy to help individuals confront and overcome relationship challenges. By integrating these methods, individuals can develop healthier thought patterns, ultimately fostering more fulfilling and harmonious relationships. Moreover, empirical evidence supports the effectiveness of CBT in improving relationship satisfaction and overall psychological well-being.

Modifying negative thought patterns in couples

One critical aspect of CBT is its efficacy in modifying negative thought patterns within couples. By addressing maladaptive thoughts and beliefs that contribute to relationship distress, CBT provides a structured framework for couples to challenge and reframe their cognitive distortions. Through techniques such as cognitive restructuring, couples can learn to identify, evaluate, and modify their negative thought patterns, fostering more constructive and positive interactions. Additionally, problem-solving strategies implemented in CBT help couples navigate conflicts and communication breakdowns effectively. By targeting these negative thought patterns, CBT equips couples with the tools needed to develop healthier perspectives, enhance relationship satisfaction, and ultimately cultivate stronger bonds. The application of CBT in couples therapy not only addresses the immediate concerns but also promotes long-lasting changes that contribute to sustained relationship well-being.

Efficacy of CBT in improving relationship satisfaction

CBT has shown significant efficacy in improving relationship satisfaction by targeting negative thought patterns. By challenging and modifying distorted beliefs and irrational thoughts, individuals undergoing CBT can enhance their communication skills, develop healthier coping mechanisms, and foster more positive interactions with their partners. Through cognitive restructuring techniques, clients can learn to identify and replace maladaptive thoughts with more rational and constructive ones, leading to improved emotional regulation and conflict resolution within relationships. Research studies have consistently demonstrated the effectiveness of CBT in treating relationship issues, highlighting its ability to bring about long-lasting positive changes in how individuals perceive and engage in their relationships. By addressing negative thought patterns at their core, CBT equips individuals with the tools necessary to cultivate healthier dynamics, fostering greater relationship satisfaction and overall well-being.

L. THE FUTURE OF PSYCHOTHERAPY

CBT stands at the forefront of modern psychotherapy, offering a systematic and structured approach to modifying negative thought patterns. Developed by pioneers like Aaron Beck and Albert Ellis, CBT is grounded in the cognitive model of psychopathology, emphasizing the interplay between thoughts, emotions, and behaviors. Through techniques like cognitive restructuring and problem-solving, CBT empowers individuals to challenge and change maladaptive beliefs, ultimately leading to improved emotional well-being. Research supports the efficacy of CBT in treating various psychological disorders, particularly depression and anxiety, by targeting and transforming negative cognitive patterns. While criticisms exist, CBT remains a potent tool in addressing negative thought patterns. Moving forward, the integration of technology, such as online platforms and virtual reality, may expand the reach and effectiveness of CBT, shaping the future of psychotherapy towards more personalized and accessible interventions for changing negative thought patterns.

The evolving landscape of mental health treatment

The evolving landscape of mental health treatment has seen a significant shift towards evidence-based interventions like CBT which focus on changing negative thought patterns. Developed by Aaron Beck and Albert Ellis, CBT operates on the premise that one's thoughts, emotions, and behaviors are interconnected, leading to maladaptive patterns. Through techniques such as cognitive restructuring, problem-solving, and exposure therapy, CBT aims to challenge and modify these negative thought patterns, enabling individuals to develop more adaptive coping strategies. Research consistently demonstrates the efficacy of CBT in treating various psychological disorders, particularly depression and anxiety. However, criticisms surrounding the accessibility and applicability of CBT persist. By critically analyzing the principles, methods, and empirical evidence of CBT, it becomes clear that this therapeutic approach holds promise in promoting positive psychological well-being by addressing and changing negative thought patterns.

CBT's place in the future of therapy

CBT is poised to become an integral part of the future of therapy due to its evidence-based approach and effectiveness in changing negative thought patterns. Originally developed by Aaron Beck and Albert Ellis in the 1960s, CBT is rooted in the cognitive model of psychopathology, which emphasizes the interconnectedness of thoughts, emotions, and behaviors. By identifying, challenging, and restructuring maladaptive thoughts, CBT helps individuals develop healthier cognitive patterns and coping strategies. Techniques such as cognitive restructuring, problem-solving, and exposure therapy are commonly employed to address negative thought distortions. Research studies have consistently shown the efficacy of CBT in treating various disorders like depression and anxiety by targeting these negative thought patterns. While some criticisms exist, such as concerns about oversimplification, CBT's emphasis on empirical validation and practical techniques make it a promising avenue for continued research and application in the field of therapy.

Innovations and challenges ahead for CBT

Innovations in CBT have been vital in adapting to the evolving therapeutic landscape, particularly in addressing the challenge of changing negative thought patterns. One key innovation lies in the integration of technology, with the rise of internet-based CBT programs offering accessible and cost-effective options for individuals seeking help. Additionally, the development of third-wave CBT approaches, such as mindfulness-based CBT and dialectical behavior therapy, has expanded the toolkit for therapists aiming to modify rigid cognitive patterns. These advancements highlight a shift towards more personalized and adaptable interventions that cater to diverse client needs. However, despite these innovations, challenges remain in ensuring the widespread dissemination and implementation of CBT techniques, especially in under-resourced settings. Moving forward, efforts to bridge this gap through telehealth services and community-based programs must be prioritized to enhance the accessibility and effectiveness of CBT interventions for individuals struggling with negative thought patterns.

LI. CONCLUSION

In conclusion, CBT stands as a powerful tool for transforming negative thought patterns, as evidenced by its widespread application and empirical support. Through the exploration of cognitive restructuring, problem-solving techniques, and exposure therapy, individuals are equipped with the skills to challenge and modify maladaptive thoughts, leading to emotional and behavioral changes. The efficacy of CBT in treating various disorders, particularly depression and anxiety, underscores its significance in promoting psychological well-being. However, despite its success, limitations and critiques surrounding CBT must be acknowledged, emphasizing the need for ongoing research and refinement. Ultimately, the ability of CBT to address negative thought patterns and promote adaptive thinking signifies a valuable contribution to the field of clinical psychology, offering a pathway towards lasting change and improved mental health outcomes. As we look to the future, further exploration and integration of CBT principles hold promise for enhancing therapeutic interventions and fostering resilience in individuals facing cognitive challenges.

Summary of key points

In summary, CBT offers a structured and evidence-based approach to modifying negative thought patterns. By understanding the interconnection between thoughts, emotions, and behaviors, CBT targets maladaptive thinking patterns that contribute to psychological distress. Through techniques like cognitive restructuring, problem-solving, and exposure therapy, individuals are guided to challenge and replace their negative thoughts with more balanced and adaptive ones. Empirical evidence supports the efficacy of CBT in treating various mental health disorders, particularly in addressing negative thought patterns associated with conditions like depression and anxiety. While CBT has demonstrated significant success, some criticisms and limitations exist, warranting further research to enhance its effectiveness. By comparing CBT with other therapeutic modalities, such as psychodynamic therapy or ACT, we can appreciate the unique strengths of CBT in facilitating lasting change in negative thought patterns, ultimately promoting psychological well-being.

Reflection on the significance of CBT in changing negative thought patterns

CBT holds immense significance in changing negative thought patterns, a fundamental aspect of psychological well-being. By delving into the core principles of CBT, individuals can identify the connection between their thoughts, emotions, and behaviors, ultimately paving the way for transformative change. Through methods like cognitive restructuring, problem-solving, and exposure techniques, CBT provides a structured framework for challenging and replacing maladaptive thought patterns with more positive and adaptive ones. The empirical evidence supporting the efficacy of CBT in treating various disorders, such as depression and anxiety, further underscores its effectiveness in reshaping negative cognitive processes. By actively engaging in CBT, individuals can gain valuable skills to navigate their thought patterns, leading to improved mental health outcomes and a greater sense of control over their thoughts and emotions. The ability of CBT to facilitate such profound changes highlights its irrefutable importance in promoting psychological well-being and fostering personal growth. This essay has explored the transformative power of CBT in challenging negative thought patterns and its lasting impact on mental health.

Future research and applications of CBT

Future research and applications of CBT hold significant promise in advancing mental health treatment. One avenue for future exploration lies in integrating technological advancements, such as virtual reality and artificial intelligence, into CBT interventions to enhance treatment efficacy. By harnessing virtual environments, therapists can simulate real-life situations for clients to confront their negative beliefs and practice adaptive coping strategies. Additionally, the development of mobile applications and online platforms tailored to deliver CBT techniques could extend therapy beyond the confines of traditional clinical settings, increasing accessibility and affordability. Moreover, investigating the efficacy of CBT in treating emerging mental health challenges, such as social media addiction or climate anxiety, could expand the scope of applications for this evidence-based therapy. Collaborative efforts between researchers, clinicians, and technology innovators will be essential to shape the future landscape of CBT and optimize its impact on changing negative thought patterns.

BIBLIOGRAPHY

Donald Meichenbaum. 'Cognitive-Behavior Modification.' An Integrative Approach, Springer Science & Business Media, 6/29/2013

Morton Hamermesh. 'Group Theory and Its Application to Physical Problems.' Courier Corporation, 4/26/2012

Denis Cooper. 'Cognitive Behavioral Therapy.' A Guide to CBT with Techniques to Cater Depression, Anxiety and Other Psychological Disorder, Gianfranco Bosi, 3/7/2021

Charles E. Schaefer. 'Play Therapy with Children.' Modalities for Change, Heidi Gerard Kaduson, American Psychological Association, 1/1/2021

Agency for Health Care Research and Quality (U.S.). 'Developing a Protocol for Observational Comparative Effectiveness Research: A User's Guide.' Government Printing Office, 2/21/2013

Rosemary B. Mennuti. 'Cognitive-Behavioral Interventions in Educational Settings.' A Handbook for Practice, Ray W. Christner, Routledge, 6/19/2013

National Research Council. 'Depression in Parents, Parenting, and Children.' Opportunities to Improve Identification, Treatment, and Prevention, Institute of Medicine, National Academies Press, 10/28/2009

Peter Armstrong. 'CBT for Depression: An Integrated Approach.' Stephen Barton, SAGE, 10/1/2018

Fernando Flores. 'Building Trust.' In Business, Politics, Relationships, and Life, Robert C. Solomon, Oxford University Press, USA, 5/1/2003

Carl Ransom Rogers. 'Client-centered Therapy.' Its Current Practice, Implications and Theory, Constable, 1/1/2003

Michael Kahn. 'Between Therapist and Client.' The New Relationship, Macmillan, 9/15/1997

Frank M. Dattilio. 'The Therapeutic Relationship in Cognitive-Behavioral Therapy.' A Clinician's Guide, Nikolaos Kazantzis, Guilford Publications, 8/7/2017

Scott O. Lilienfeld. 'The Encyclopedia of Clinical Psychology, 5 Volume Set.' Robin L. Cautin, John Wiley & Sons, 1/20/2015

World Health Organization. 'Adherence to Long-term Therapies.' Evidence for Action, Eduardo Sabaté, World Health Organization, 1/1/2003

Arbind Kumar Jha. 'Homework EducationA Powerful Tool Of Learning.' Atlantic Publishers & Dist, 1/1/2006

Frank P. Deane. 'Using Homework Assignments in Cognitive Behavior Therapy.' Nikolaos Kazantzis, Routledge, 12/5/2005

Mary Beth Harris. 'The School Practitioner's Concise Companion to Health and Well Being.' Cynthia Franklin, OUP USA, 1/1/2008

The School of Life. 'What is Psychotherapy?.' Duckworth Books, 5/17/2018

Ted McCain. 'Teaching for Tomorrow.' Teaching Content and Problem-Solving Skills, Corwin Press, 2/1/2005

Arthur M. Nezu, PhD, ABPP. 'Problem-Solving Therapy.' A Positive Approach to Clinical Intervention, Third Edition, Thomas D'Zurilla, PhD, Springer Publishing Company, 9/18/2006

Andrew M. Busch. 'Behavioral Activation.' Distinctive Features, Jonathan W. Kanter, Routledge, 5/7/2009

Mark B. Powers. 'Personalized Exposure Therapy.' A Person-Centered Transdiagnostic Approach, Jasper A. J. Smits, Oxford University Press, 1/1/2019

Khadj Rouf. 'Oxford Guide to Behavioural Experiments in Cognitive Therapy.' OUP Oxford, 5/6/2004

Alexander L. Chapman. 'Behavioral Interventions in Cognitive Behavior Therapy.' Practical Guidance for Putting Theory Into Action, Richard F. Farmer, American Psychological Association, 1/1/2016

Derek Truscott. 'Cognitive-behavioral Therapy for Refractory Cases.' Turning Failure Into Success, American Psychological Association, 1/1/2010

Wilford Johnson. 'Navigating Negative Thoughts Guide.' Techniques To Challenge And Overcome Negative Thought Patterns, Amazon Digital Services LLC - Kdp, 7/29/2023

Raymond Aisabor. 'Understanding Your Purpose.' Lulu.com, 12/31/2014

Stefan G. Hofmann. 'CBT For Anxiety Disorders.' A Practitioner Book, Gregoris Simos, John Wiley & Sons, 3/5/2013

J. Rick Turner. 'Encyclopedia of Behavioral Medicine.' Marc D. Gellman, Springer New York, 1/1/2019

Carolyn Jarvis. 'Study Guide & Laboratory Manual for Physical Examination & Health Assessment E-Book.' Elsevier Health Sciences, 1/20/2019

Allan Tasman. 'Less Time to Do More.' Psychotherapy on the Short-term Inpatient Unit, Ellen Leibenluft, American Psychiatric Pub, 1/1/1993

Hannie van Genderen. 'Breaking Negative Thinking Patterns.' A Schema Therapy Self-Help and Support Book, Gitta Jacob, John Wiley & Sons, 3/16/2015

Corinne Sweet. 'Change Your Life With CBT.' How Cognitive Behavioural Therapy Can Transform Your Life, Pearson UK, 9/26/2012

Michael Townend. 'Cognitive Behavioural Therapy in Mental Health Care.' Alec Grant, SAGE, 2/17/2010

Frank M. Dattilio. 'The Therapeutic Relationship in Cognitive-Behavioral Therapy.' A Clinician's Guide, Nikolaos Kazantzis, Guilford Publications, 6/27/2017

Jane E. Fisher. 'Cognitive Behavior Therapy.' Core Principles for Practice, William T. O'Donohue, John Wiley & Sons, 6/13/2012

David D. Burns. 'Feeling Good.' The New Mood Therapy, Penguin, 1/1/1981

Anthony R. Ciminero. 'Maladaptive Behavior.' An Introduction to Abnormal Psychology, Benjamin B. Lahey, Scott, Foresman, 1/1/1980

Henry Kellerman. 'Theories of Emotion.' Robert Plutchik, Academic Press, 10/22/2013

Aaron T. Beck. 'Scientific Foundations of Cognitive Theory and Therapy of Depression.' David A. Clak, John Wiley & Sons, 4/30/1999

Philip C. Kendall. 'Psychopathology and Cognition.' Keith S. Dobson, Academic Press, 1/1/1993

Source Wikipedia. 'Cognitive Therapy.' Aaron T. Beck, Academy of Cognitive Therapy, Albert Ellis, Arbitrary Inference, Bessel Van Der Kolk, Cognitive Analytic Therapy, Co, General Books, 9/1/2013

Donald Meichenbaum. 'The Evolution of Cognitive Behavior Therapy.' A Personal and Professional Journey with Don Meichenbaum, Taylor & Francis, 2/17/2017

Paul Grant. 'Recovery-Oriented Cognitive Therapy for Serious Mental Health Conditions.' Aaron T. Beck, Guilford Publications, 12/8/2020

M.D. Naomi M. Simon. '10-Minute CBT.' Integrating Cognitive-Behavioral Strategies Into Your Practice, Ph.D. Michael W. Otto, Oxford University Press, 5/1/2011

Loretta Graziano Breuning. 'The Science of Positivity.' Stop Negative Thought Patterns by Changing Your Brain Chemistry, Simon and Schuster, 12/2/2016

Freda McManus. 'Cognitive Behavioural Therapy.' A Very Short Introduction, Oxford University Press, 1/1/2022